29 / PART 2

August 2013

Commissioned by **David Spriggs***; edited by* **Lisa Cherrett**

Guidelines © BRF 2013

The Bible Reading Fellowship
15 The Chambers, Vineyard, Abingdon OX14 3FE
Tel: 01865 319700; Fax: 01865 319701
E-mail: enquiries@brf.org.uk; Website: www.brf.org.uk

ISBN 978 1 84101 764 8

Distributed in Australia by Mediacom Education Inc., PO Box 610, Unley, SA 5061.
Tel: 1800 811 311; Fax: 08 8297 8719;
E-mail: admin@mediacom.org.au
Available also from all good Christian bookshops in Australia.
For individual and group subscriptions in Australia:
Mrs Rosemary Morrall, PO Box W35, Wanniassa, ACT 2903.

Distributed in New Zealand by Scripture Union Wholesale, PO Box 760, Wellington
Tel: 04 385 0421; Fax: 04 384 3990; E-mail: suwholesale@clear.net.nz

Publications distributed to more than 60 countries

Acknowledgments
The New Revised Standard Version of the Bible, Anglicised Edition, copyright © 1989, 1995 by the
Division of Christian Education of the National Council of the Churches of Christ in the USA.
Used by permission. All rights reserved.

The Holy Bible, New International Version, Anglicised Edition, copyright © 1979, 1984, 2011
by Biblica (formerly International Bible Society). Used by permission of Hodder & Stoughton
Publishers, an Hachette UK company. All rights reserved. 'NIV' is a registered trademark of
International Bible Society. UK trademark number 1448790.

The New Jerusalem Bible, published and copyright © 1985 by Darton, Longman and Todd Ltd and
les Editions du Cerf, and by Doubleday, a division of Bantam Doubleday Dell Publishing Group,
Inc. Used by permission of Darton, Longman and Todd Ltd, and Doubleday, a division of Random
house, Inc.

Scripture quotations from THE MESSAGE. Copyright © by Eugene H. Peterson 1993, 1994, 1995.
Used by permission of NavPress Publishing Group.

Revised Grail Psalms copyright © 2008, Conception Abbey/The Grail, admin. by GIA Publications,
Inc., www.giamusic.com. All rights reserved.

Printed in Singapore by Craft Print International Ltd

Suggestions for using *Guidelines*

Set aside a regular time and place, if possible, when you can read and pray undisturbed. Before you begin, take time to be still and, if you find it helpful, use the BRF prayer.

In *Guidelines*, the introductory section provides context for the passages or themes to be studied, while the units of comment can be used daily, weekly, or whatever best fits your timetable. You will need a Bible (more than one if you want to compare different translations) as Bible passages are not included. At the end of each week is a 'Guidelines' section, offering further thoughts about, or practical application of what you have been studying.

You may find it helpful to keep a journal to record your thoughts about your study, or to note items for prayer. Another way of using *Guidelines* is to meet with others to discuss the material, either regularly or occasionally.

Occasionally, you may read something in *Guidelines* that you find particularly challenging, even uncomfortable. This is inevitable in a series of notes which draws on a wide spectrum of contributors, and doesn't believe in ducking difficult issues. Indeed, we believe that *Guidelines* readers much prefer thought-provoking material to a bland diet that only confirms what they already think.

If you do disagree with a contributor, you may find it helpful to go through these three steps. First, think about why you feel uncomfortable. Perhaps this is an idea that is new to you, or you are not happy at the way something has been expressed. Or there may be something more substantial—you may feel that the writer is guilty of sweeping generalisation, factual error, theological or ethical misjudgment. Second, pray that God would use this disagreement to teach you more about his word and about yourself. Third, think about what you will do as a result of the disagreement. You might resolve to find out more about the issue, or write to the contributor or the editors of *Guidelines*. After all, we aim to be 'doers of the word', not just people who hold opinions about it.

Writers in this issue

Derek Tidball is a Baptist minister who was principal of London School of Theology (formerly London Bible College) for twelve years. A frequent Bible conference speaker and prolific author, Derek has written *The Message of Leviticus* for IVP's 'Bible Speaks Today' series. He lives in Leicester where he is on the leadership team of Whetstone Baptist Church.

P.W. (Bill) Goodman is a teacher, writer and Anglican clergyman living in Leicestershire. He loves helping people explore the Bible in different cultural contexts. His recent PhD set contemporary songs in conversation with biblical songs.

David Spriggs is a Baptist minister who has worked for the last 15 years with Bible Society, helping the churches and Higher Education to engage more fruitfully with the Bible. His passion is to see Christians enjoying their faith more and growing in their love for God and people.

Antony Billington is Head of Theology at London Institute for Contemporary Christianity, having formerly taught hermeneutics and biblical theology at London School of Theology. He is the author, with Margaret Killingray and Helen Parry, of *Whole Life, Whole Bible* (BRF, 2012).

Henry Wansbrough OSB is a monk at Ampleforth Abbey in Yorkshire. He is Executive Secretary of the International Commission for Producing an English-Language Lectionary (ICPEL) for the Roman Catholic Church, and lectures frequently across the globe.

Andrew Watson is the Bishop of Aston, having previously led three churches in Redditch, Notting Hill and Twickenham, and planted several more. He is the author of *The Fourfold Leadership of Jesus*, *Confidence in the Living God* and *The Way of the Desert*, all published by BRF.

Janet Fletcher is Team Vicar in the Rectorial Benefice of Bangor. She offers spiritual direction and enjoys teaching groups in prayer, faith and spirituality, and leading quiet days. She has written *Pathway to God* (SPCK, 2006) and has contributed to BRF's prayer and spirituality journal, *Quiet Spaces*.

Steve Holmes is Senior Lecturer in Systematic Theology at the University of St Andrews. A regular speaker at Christian conferences, he offers theological consultancy to Christian organisations engaged in public policy work. He chairs the Theology and Public Policy Advisory Commission for the Evangelical Alliance.

The Editor writes...

Guidelines has an enviable and well-warranted reputation of supplying intelligent and insightful comments to elucidate the biblical text and provide substantial inspiration for our spiritual journey. This reputation has been enhanced by the Revd Dr Jeremy Duff who has served us as commissioning editor. As Jeremy lays down this role, on behalf of all our readers I want to say a huge thank you to him. We recognise with thanksgiving our debt of gratitude to him for maintaining the quality and ensuring freshness and relevance—the best of old and new.

This edition continues that process. Some of the writers are part of the riches of the old. Fr Henry Wansbrough continues his guided tour through the Psalms and Janet Fletcher opens up for us the fruit of the Spirit as part of our post-Pentecost meditations. Andrew Watson may be new to *Guidelines* but he has already written several books for BRF. Here we have some of his most incisive insights on Christian leadership today, in the light of Christ's ministry.

There are, however, some new contributors. Steve Holmes of St Andrews University (yes, the meeting place of the Duke and Duchess of Cambridge!) brings his understanding of systematic theology to interplay with biblical texts as he explores some of the Bible's teaching on the Holy Spirit. Antony Billington of the London Institute for Contemporary Christianity (LICC) opens up some Old Testament insights on wisdom, while Bill Goodman explores the little gem of 2 Peter.

Then there are Derek Tidball and myself! Derek is both old and new, as he wrote for *Guidelines* some time ago, as is true for me. Derek takes us into the strange world of Leviticus but, perhaps surprisingly for some, enables us to see its profound value for Christians today. I continue my contribution on Luke's Gospel, as well as one week of readings considering the *Missio Dei* in the light of the Acts of the Apostles.

Taken together, here is a rich diet. Frequently both Old and New Testaments feature in the same set of notes, for as Christians we regard both Testaments together as one book. The whole of this amazing text is fundamental to all that is provided in these notes. As we engage with the Bible prayerfully and responsively, the notes serve best their noble purpose.

I look forward to serving you all over the next few editions.

David Spriggs
Commissioning Editor

The BRF Prayer

Almighty God,
you have taught us that your word is a lamp for our
feet and a light for our path. Help us, and all who
prayerfully read your word, to deepen our
fellowship with you and with each other through your love.
And in so doing may we come to know you more fully,
love you more truly, and follow more faithfully in
the steps of your son Jesus Christ, who lives and
reigns with you and the Holy Spirit,
one God for evermore. Amen.

Leviticus

While, for many people, Leviticus is an unopened book, it lays important foundations for our understanding of the Christian faith and life. Its first 16 chapters (which we shall study over the next week) introduce Israel's sacrificial worship and the origin of the Aaronic priesthood, both of which come to completion in Jesus, who is the ultimate sacrifice and great high priest. These chapters are therefore no longer directly relevant for Christians, yet they continue to provide significant insights into Christ's work and into our approach to worship. They instructed Israel on how to distinguish itself from other nations by the adoption of special food laws. They also taught how to distinguish between what was ritually clean and unclean, holy and common, and how to repair the situation when people or things were contaminated. In all this, God was teaching his people about himself, their identity and the meaning of holiness, although he did so by using dramatic symbolic action and analogy rather than explicitly by using propositions. He wanted them to be holy as he is holy (11:45), and to exhibit him in their behaviour and lifestyles.

Jewish schools began teaching the Torah (the first five books of the Bible) with Leviticus because it taught the students how to live, before explaining why they were to adopt this identity in the retelling of their story.

The second half of the highly organised book of Leviticus (to which we shall turn in our second week of study) is generally known as the 'holiness code'. Leviticus 17—26 is not primarily concerned with the rituals and sacrifices that occupy the first part of the book, but with how people are to behave as members of God's special community. Chapter 17 links back to the food laws but, after that, the holiness code covers a wide range of issues, including penal policy, family and sexual ethics, principles of business and social relationships, the treatment of the poor and immigrants, expectations of leaders, and details of its annual calendar. It sometimes teaches Israel how to live by laying down broad principles and sometimes by giving specific examples. The 'laws' do not function like our modern criminal law does, but they do build a clear picture of the sort of community (and therefore what sort of people) God wanted.

Chapter 26 summarises the terms of the 'covenant'. Some scholars see chapter 27 as an appendix but its details actually contain a significant lesson: God is not to be cheated by his people but is worthy of full homage.

1 Voluntary offerings

Leviticus 1:1–13; 2:1–13; 3:1–17

Israel was primarily a worshipping community, but Israel's God was not dependent on receiving offerings from his people. It was he who generously provided for them rather than needing to receive from them. When Israel offered sacrifices, they were not doing God a favour—which is why not just any offering would be acceptable, however well-intentioned. As a result, Leviticus insists that sacrifices are to be offered in particular ways. It is important to get them right also because the rituals illustrate spiritual truths.

Since worship is central, Leviticus begins with instructions about the offerings by first addressing all the people (1:1—6:7) and then going back over the same ground to give the officiating priests some additional instructions (6:8—7:38). One of the impressive things about these instructions is their inclusivity. Women as well as men were included in the 'anyone' of 1:2, and poor people sacrificed alongside the rich. If someone could not afford to offer an animal from the flock, a dove or pigeon would suffice, so sacrifices were within everyone's reach (1:10–17).

Three offerings were voluntary. The burnt offering (1:1–16; see also 6:8–13) served as the basic all-purpose offering of Israel, being presented by the whole community every morning and evening, and occasionally also by individuals. The fire's total consumption of the offering symbolised the fact that Israel belonged wholly to God.

The grain offering (2:1–16; see also 6:14–23) could take a number of forms, all of which included the use of oil (basic to cooking, and later symbolising the Holy Spirit) and salt, a symbol of the people's covenant with God (Numbers 18:19). Two forms included incense; but yeast and honey, which could cause fermentation and so change the basic nature of the original ingredients, were forbidden. The offering was a way of offering the fruit of one's natural labour to God and of providing 'an aroma pleasing to the Lord' (2:2, 9, 12).

The fellowship offering (3:1–17; see also 7:11–21) goes under a number of names, of which 'peace offering' is probably best, both because its Hebrew name relates to the word *shalom* (peace) and because it celebrates the well-being that God gives to people. The best parts of the animal (the fat and kidneys) were reserved for God, but the rest served to provide food for a communal feast.

Sacrifices expressed Israel's warm relationship with their gracious covenant God.

2 Compulsory offerings

Leviticus 4:1–31; 5:1–6, 14–19; 6:1–7

If the burnt, grain and fellowship (or peace) offerings were voluntary, another two were required in certain circumstances. They were the means by which atonement was made when the people sinned or proved unfaithful to God. Failure to offer them would mean that the rupture in their relationship with God would not be repaired.

The sin offering (4:1—5:13; see also 6:24–30) would not cover sins that were committed in deliberate defiance against God, but it would cover all inadvertent sins and those where an Israelite had tried but failed to measure up to the exacting standards of personal integrity or social and spiritual responsibility that were required of them (5:1–4). The offering usually required an unblemished animal sacrifice to serve as a substitute for the wrongdoer, prefiguring the atoning sacrifice of Christ on the cross. An unusual feature, however, was that the offering was graded, with priests having to offer the most costly sacrifice, leaders the next most costly, and ordinary people the least expensive of all, according to their circumstances. If they were really poor, they need only bring a cup of flour (5:11–13) and they would be forgiven. Thus God showed himself to be rich in mercy.

The guilt offering (5:14—6:7; see also 7:1–10) also secured atonement for sin but it differed from the sin offering. Not only was it demanded when particular sins were committed (those of sacrilege, disobedience to

God and deception or failing of one's neighbour) but it also required that, in addition to the sacrifice, reparation for one's wrongdoing was made. The guilty party was required not only to restore lost, damaged or stolen property but also to add a 20 per cent fine to its value (6:5), and all this was to be done before the sacrifice could be offered. In this way, God was teaching Israel that although atonement was readily available, it was not to be gained casually. Sin costs and atonement has its price.

The rituals were designed to ensure that the sinner took seriously the offering of a substitute for their sin. They were required to lay their hands on the animal, slaughter it, and confess their sin over it. Grace is free but it is not cheap.

3 Enter the priests

Leviticus 8:1—9:7, 22–24; 10:1–3

As we have seen, at the heart of Israel's worship lay the sacrifices. Consequently a priesthood was required—people trained and commissioned to present the offerings to God. The work of the priests was wider than just serving as liturgical celebrants. They also had to make crucial judgments about what was holy (set apart for God) and what was available for common use, and they had to instruct the people in God's law (10:10–11).

Aaron's family were selected to serve as priests and were installed in an elaborate celebration that lasted a week. Until their ordination was complete, Moses took charge and offered the sacrifices. Several factors were involved, with the outward actions signifying spiritual realities. Aaron and his sons were bathed (8:6) as a sign of cleansing. They were clothed (vv. 7–9), their 'uniform' signalling both their responsibilities and the dignity of their position. They were anointed (vv. 10–12), the sign of consecration to office and of divine empowerment. Sacrifices were offered on their behalf (vv. 14–30) to atone for their sin and symbolise their complete availability to God. Only then, 'on the eighth day', the day of new beginnings, was Aaron able to offer sacrifices himself (9:1–23), which God dramatically accepted (v. 24). All this was done very publicly, perhaps to overcome any doubts that people may have had about Aaron after the incident with the golden calf (Exodus 32) and to ensure that they would all respect him. God is in the restoration business.

No sooner had Aaron and his family assumed their responsibilities, however, than it all went tragically wrong. His sons, Nadab and Abihu, 'offered unauthorised fire before the Lord' (10:1). We do not know what made this offering illegitimate. Several explanations have been advanced, all of which have merit: perhaps they were playing around, used the wrong ingredients, were drunk, trespassed on the Most Holy Place, and so on. Whatever the explanation, they paid for their unworthy approach to God, as their lives were taken by fire (v. 2; contrast this with the fire in 9:24). It was a severe lesson, but serving God requires the utmost care and the most exacting obedience. Casual attitudes have no place in spiritual leadership.

While lessons may be drawn from these early days of the Aaronic priesthood for contemporary pastoral leadership, Christians now have a great high priest who has rendered a human priesthood redundant (Hebrews 4:14—5:10).

4 Israel's diet

Leviticus 11

Although, with globalisation, it is less true than it was, food is a distinguishing marker for individual nations. We only have to think about English fish and chips, Scottish haggis, Indian curries, Italian pasta and American hamburgers to make the point. Israel was no exception, and certain foods were declared 'clean' and therefore edible, and others 'unclean' and so not to be eaten.

Much effort has been expended in trying to explain what determined whether a land animal, sea creature, flying creature or insect was clean or not. Some commentators have detected health benefits in the prescribed diet. Others, more persuasively, have seen the differences as symbolic of the way the community itself should function. The animals considered clean were those that conformed most naturally to the expectations for their class of creature. Animals might be expected to have divided hooves and chew the cud, and fish to have fins and scales—so those that did not have these characteristics were 'unclean'. Birds that prey on blood, and insects that swarm, defying the normal categories of motion, were also judged 'unclean'. In this way, even in the kitchen, Israel was being taught a lesson about its identity as God's holy people. Holiness involved wholeness, completeness, integrity and unity.

The only explanation the Bible itself gives for these regulations is that they are to do with holiness (vv. 43–45). To be holy is to be 'set apart' from the ordinary for the service of God and to live in obedience to his commands. So, for all their mystery, perhaps nothing more lies behind these dietary regulations than God's command that the Israelites were to mark themselves off as a distinct people and culture, separate from the nations around them and devoted exclusively to him.

We might add a footnote. By labelling some creatures 'unclean' or 'detestable', the regulations were not saying that these animals were inherently disgusting. Paradoxically, the label resulted in their preservation and protection: since they could not be killed for food, they were allowed to flourish while other species were endangered.

God's people no longer distinguish themselves by observing particular food laws (Mark 7:17–22; Acts 10:9–23) but by their moral and virtuous behaviour.

5 Clean and unclean

Leviticus 12:1–8; 13:1–8, 47–52; 14:1–20, 33–53; 15:1–15
These chapters, which extend the regulations about what is clean and unclean beyond food to areas of health and housing, are considered by many to be the most arcane and inaccessible in the whole of Leviticus. That's a curious reaction, given that the world in which we live is riddled with many more burdensome and detailed health and safety regulations, covering more aspects of life than those found here. All societies have such regulations but these are given by God (12:1; 13:1; 14:1, 33; 15:1) and convey spiritual truth. They relate to ritual impurity rather than moral impurities or sin, and the connection between them is about what to do when the 'walls' are breached, whether they are 'walls' of the body, garments or the home.

The first regulations (ch. 12) ensure that mothers are given time to recover after childbirth before resuming active life, courtesy of a burnt offering. The next regulations (13:1–46) concern various skin diseases that break out and crack open the skin (probably not leprosy as has traditionally been thought). The priest had to determine how serious the disease was. Serious eruptions and rashes led to a person being excluded from the community until they had recovered.

Regulations follow about mould in leather and garments (13:47–59) or in houses (14:33–57). Again, courses of action are prescribed according to the severity of the problem. Finally, attention is given to discharges from the human body, of an 'unusual' kind due to illness or of a natural or sexual kind (ch. 15). Any discharge breaks through the body's walls and contaminates not only the person themselves but also any objects that are in contact. Rituals to restore normality and heal the rupture are set out.

Unlike Jesus, priests had no way of healing people, only of monitoring their progress and restoring them once healing had occurred. Central to these chapters are the rituals that enabled a previously unclean person to re-enter the community (14:1–32). The rituals uniquely involved two birds (one of which was killed and the other released), a careful physical examination, and the offering of the normal burnt, sin and guilt offerings. Finally, the person was anointed to serve in the community again. In this way they were (in the words of the hymn) 'ransomed, healed, restored, forgiven'.

There is some obvious health benefit in these regulations, which are appropriate to more primitive times, but they also symbolically teach God's desire for wholeness and lack of any rupture among his people.

6 The greatest day of the year

Leviticus 16

The annual Day of Atonement was the greatest day in Israel's calendar. The whole community was to prepare for it by self-denial and then to celebrate it, because what was enacted on that day affected everyone (vv. 29–33). Its importance was underlined by the date on which it occurred (the tenth day of the seventh, most sacred, month), by the unique and complex rituals it involved, and by the fact that the instructions for its celebration were placed at this pivotal point in the book of Leviticus.

Sacrifices were offered throughout the year for particular sins, but on this day a great spiritual spring-cleaning took place that resulted in atonement being made for 'all' the sins of the people. The high priest had to make careful preparation for the central acts of the day, which included dressing in simple robes and offering sacrifices for his own sin before daring to represent others.

At the heart of the day were two goats (vv. 15–22). One was to pay the price of people's sins by being sacrificed as their substitute, its blood being sprinkled on the cover of the ark of the covenant in the Most Holy Place. This was the only day of the year when anyone went into this innermost part of the tabernacle, and special protective measures had to be taken to ensure the high priest's safety in the presence of God's awesome holiness. The second goat—the scapegoat—had the people's sins confessed over it and transferred to it. The goat then bore those sins away to the desert, the unclean place outside the camp. Their sins were gone for ever, never to trouble them again.

This was a graphic and dramatic way of demonstrating God's dealing with sin and removing it from people (see Psalm 103:12). The atonement ritual also meant that God's own dwelling-place was cleansed, enabling him to reside in peace again among his people. After the rituals, the high priest was to observe a sequence of withdrawal as careful as the sequence he had observed when approaching God.

The God of Israel was an awesome God, not to be treated lightly, and yet, simultaneously, he was a God of abounding grace who took the initiative in making it possible for people's sins to be completely forgiven. The God of Israel is our God, 'the God and Father of our Lord Jesus Christ' (Ephesians 1:3).

Guidelines

Reflect on this week's chapters by asking the following questions.

- What were the varied reasons for people to offer sacrifices? What do they teach me about God and my approach to worship? Is my worship as varied, careful, wholehearted and atoning as theirs?

- Noting the careful approach taken to Aaron's ordination as a priest, what implications may this have for believers in Christ, who are all priests of the new covenant (1 Peter 2:9)?
- Israel's distinctive identity was enshrined in its dietary laws. Can you list some of the important ways in which God's people today should be distinguishable from others.
- The purity regulations demonstrate a concern for integrity and wholeness, a horror of impurity, and a way of handling and overcoming uncleanness and restoring wholeness. Are we as passionate about the desire for holiness, and what steps do we take to pursue it in our lives?
- In what ways does the Day of Atonement anticipate the death of Jesus Christ on the cross? In what ways is Jesus like both the goat that shed its blood and the scapegoat (John 1:29)?

1 Family life and sexual sins

Leviticus 18 and 20

These are among the most maligned chapters in Leviticus. Their condemnation of homosexual practice and apparent advocacy of capital punishment is out of step with contemporary liberal culture. Those who dismiss them, though, often do so tritely, failing to understand their positive intent. Both chapters are concerned with how the Israelites were to build stable families, the basic building blocks of any healthy community and society. This would be achieved by remaining faithful to their God and by adopting a different lifestyle from the nations around them: such was the path to life (18:1–5).

Chapter 18 concerns behaviour that would undermine the integrity of the family. Verses 6–17 deal with the question of incest, setting out the various close blood relations between whom sexual relationships were forbidden. These verses are followed by two notes (vv. 18–19) instructing men to act wisely and with consideration towards their wives. Then, verses 20–30 ban four practices that equally undermine families and are inconsistent with God's intention for marriage, as set out in Genesis 2:24

and constantly affirmed elsewhere. The practices are adultery (v. 20), child sacrifice, which was commonly practised elsewhere (v. 21), homosexual relations (v. 22: not what we understand as homosexual orientation) and bestiality (v. 23). These patterns of healthy living had to apply to all who lived among the Israelites, even immigrants, and would lead to a settled and contented existence in the land.

Chapter 20 largely follows through the implications of chapter 18. What is Israel to do if people offend against these ethical rules? Four kinds of punishment are stipulated, ranging from execution accompanied by God's strongest disapproval (vv. 2–6), execution by the community (vv. 9–16) and banishment (vv. 17–18) to God's imposition of childlessness (vv. 20–21). The penalties bear witness to the truth that living God's way leads to life, whereas rejecting his path leads to death. They testify to the seriousness of sin and to the way humans must accept responsibility for their actions. The purpose of these rules is not to encourage punitive attitudes but rather to encourage people in holy living (20:7–8, 22–26).

2 A great ethical charter

Leviticus 19

I was talking with a liberal Jewish rabbi who was scathing about Leviticus and saw no room for it in modern Judaism—except, he said, for chapters 19 and 25, the most wonderful ethical chapters in the Old Testament. He was right about these two chapters, if not about the rest.

Leviticus 19 suffers from being regarded by many as a collection of 'various laws' thrown together in a random fashion. That's not quite accurate. Verse 2 serves as a title for the whole chapter, which is concerned throughout with inviting Israel to 'be holy because I, the Lord your God, am holy'. The people of Israel are to be his mirror image in the world, reflecting his goodness, purity and grace in their dealings with others. The use of different terminology (obscured by our English translations) marks out three sections, composed of foundational issues in verses 1–10, short commands in verses 11–18, and the 'decrees' of verses 19–37.

Several factors are noticeable. The chapter makes no distinction between 'spiritual' matters (for example, vv. 4–8) and social issues (for example, vv. 9, 13). Both are concerned with holiness, and there is no hierarchy of sins. What happens in the family, the field and the factory matters as much to God as what happens in the place of worship. The laws address feelings (vv. 17–18) and motives, not just actions. Sometimes they teach through concrete examples (vv. 14, 32) and sometimes by reference to general principles (v. 33). Occasionally the commands make sense only in the light of practices at the time: for example, verses 27 and 28 are not really concerned with modern 'body art' but call Israel to eschew the mourning rituals of neighbouring nations. Throughout, there is a concern that all people, whether they are relatives, neighbours, business associates, disabled, elderly, slaves or immigrants, should be treated with dignity.

Leviticus 19 is about how to create a wholesome society. It is a commentary on the two greatest commandments—to love God with all that you are and to love your neighbour as yourself (Luke 10:27). Indeed, the second of these commandments finds its origin in Leviticus 19:18.

3 The obligations of spiritual leaders

Leviticus 21 and 22

Leaders set the tone in any society and, for much of Israel's life—both before the establishment of the monarchy and after its downfall—'leaders' meant the priests. Consequently, these chapters contain what we today would describe as the person specification and professional code of conduct for priests.

The basic requirement was that priests should demonstrate their total dedication to the Lord: 'They must be holy to their God' (21:6). Such single-minded devotion would show itself in the way they mourned (vv. 1–6). Touching a corpse rendered a person unclean, so a priest who did so, or adopted signs of grief that were common elsewhere, would be unavailable for duty. Priests' right to mourn was therefore severely restricted. Not all women were suitable marriage partners, so the priests' dedication to God was also to be reflected in their choice of partner (v. 7). Rules that applied to the ordinary priests were even more stringently applied to the high priest (vv. 10–15), reflecting his greater responsibilities and closeness to God.

Priests were also required to be free from any physical disability (vv. 16–23). Today we see this as unacceptable discrimination, but then it was a way of teaching that only the best was good enough for God. Animal sacrifices needed to be unblemished; so too did the priests who offered them. For us as Christians, these restrictions no longer apply, since Christ alone is the unblemished priest who offered himself as a perfect sacrifice. He fulfilled the intention of these rules as the healer who brings wholeness to the unclean and leads the excluded into his kingdom.

Chapter 22 contains the priests' professional code of practice. It warns them not to cut corners when they serve God. The priest who thinks his skin disease doesn't matter should think again (vv. 1–9). The priest who stretches the rules and becomes too lenient with the regulations about who might eat sacrifices is accountable to God (vv. 10–16). Sacrifices had to be of an acceptable standard (vv. 17–30), and God was not fooled if people sought to pass off sub-standard offerings, even if they were voluntary. All this teaches us that good intentions are not enough. The fact that the priests meant well meant nothing if they offered less than perfect obedience to God. That's an important lesson for those who lead congregational worship in contemporary culture.

4 The calendar of celebration

Leviticus 23:1—24:9

The more we succumb to a 24/7 society, the more we learn about the importance of a rhythm in life, where work is balanced by rest and space for recreation. That is why the sabbath is so important in scripture. Although religious folk have sometimes turned it into an oppressive regime of boredom, its original intention was to prevent people from working non-stop. It was a day set aside to focus on God, to discover the rhythm that he built into his creation. When Israel was instructed about its festivals, the weekly observance of the sabbath was mentioned first of all (23:3)

Societies need more than this weekly rhythm, however. They need an annual calendar as well. Every culture has its special holidays, which sometimes commemorate some great event in its history. Israel was no exception. Its numerous feasts usually conveyed a fairly transparent spiritual lesson. The Passover celebrated the exodus from Egypt and was perhaps Israel's greatest festival of all (vv. 4–5), equivalent to Thanksgiving Day in the USA or Liberation Days held elsewhere in the world. The Passover merged into the feast of Unleavened Bread (vv. 6–8), which Paul used as a metaphor for instructing Christians to get rid of evil in their lives (1 Corinthians 5:7).

Other festivals were related to the agricultural year. The offering of Firstfruits celebrated the start of the barley harvest (vv. 9–14), whereas the feast of Weeks celebrated its conclusion (vv. 15–22). These festivals mark a recognition that God is the provider. The seventh month was a light month in the fields, so it offered time to feast. The first autumn festival was the feast of Trumpets (vv. 23–25). In the same month, the Day of Atonement was re-enacted (vv. 26–32), recalling God's complete forgiveness. The agricultural year was brought to a climax with the feast of Tabernacles, a feast that figured large in the life of Jesus, who claimed to be its fulfilment (John 7:37–38).

These celebrations would have been the high points of the year. Perhaps it is no accident that instructions about them are followed by instructions about routine and unremarkable service in the tabernacle (24:1–9). God is to be honoured in both the ordinary and the exceptional.

5 Proclaim liberty

Leviticus 25

Astonishingly, it was this obscure chapter of Leviticus that inspired the Jubilee campaign which did so much to change attitudes towards Third World debt at the turn of the millennium. We see again how Israel's faith was a perfect blend of the spiritual and the practical, the God-centred and the human-focused. The concern throughout is that the land and its people should live in freedom, and the means by which they would do so was expressed in the sabbath principle.

Anxiety about producing enough food for everyone could easily lead the people of Israel to farm their lands relentlessly and so denude them of all nutrients. Just as people were to take time out, then, so every seventh year was to be a rest year for the soil (vv. 1–7). Of its own accord, it would produce enough during that year for the Israelites to eat. Although people might understand that rationally, however, keeping this law would still require great trust in God, since the human disposition is always to feel the need to work and earn our keep.

The same principle of freedom runs through the rest of the chapter, which introduces the Jubilee year, a sabbath of sabbaths. What happened if a fellow Israelite fell on hard times? How could they get out of poverty? A series of steps is outlined in verses 25–55, any of which might restore the poor to their home and property. If all else failed, however, every 50th year was to be a special year in which liberty was proclaimed throughout the land (vv. 9–10). That year, all debts would be cancelled and all those in debt would return to their homes and lands. They were not condemned to perpetual slavery.

Deep convictions undergirded the Jubilee legislation, concerning the integrity of family life and the importance of home, but also the understanding that nobody actually owned land, since it all belonged to God (vv. 23–24). The Israelite's role was to steward it wisely on God's behalf. With good reason, many see Jesus as bringing this Jubilee principle to fulfilment, as he sets people free from the many powers that imprison them (see Luke 4:16–21).

6 To sum up

Leviticus 26

The tone with which we speak sometimes matters as much as the words we say. The same words can sound threatening or promising. All too often, people hear the wrong tone when reading Leviticus. The constant repetition of 'I am the Lord you God', or some such phrase, can sound menacing, as if God is saying, 'I'm in charge: do this or else.' Nothing could, in fact, be further from the truth. God's constant reference to himself in this way is a reminder that he is Israel's covenant God, the one who has chosen the Israelites as his special people, has delivered them from oppression in Egypt and will continue to protect them in a hostile world. But covenants involve two parties, not one, and the Israelites were expected to adopt a certain lifestyle as a result, one that would reflect God's character.

Covenant treaties that set out the expectations on both sides were customary in the ancient world, and we have a summary of the treaty between God and Israel in this penultimate chapter of Leviticus. The longer version is found in Deuteronomy 28—30. (In fact, some scholars see the whole of Deuteronomy as a covenant document.)

Verses 1–13 set out what God will do for the Israelites if they observe their side of the agreement. They can expect God to provide for them, grant them peace, lead them to prosperity, protect them and be present among them. On the other hand, should they choose to ignore God's commands and live by their own rules, they cannot expect to experience the blessings he has promised. Verses 14–46, then, outline the other side of the coin. Their disobedience to God's laws will lead to a withdrawal of his blessing, gently at first in the hope that a nudge will remind them of their agreement, but with increasing severity, until God's presence is withdrawn from them totally.

Sadly, the warnings went unheeded and the Israelites experienced not the life God longed to give them but defeat at the hand of their enemies— for the ten northern tribes, complete destruction by the Assyrians and, for many in the southern tribes, the living death of exile in Babylon. Yet, like a flower breaking through the hardened, snow-clad soil of winter, the gospel keeps poking through the curses. 'If they will confess… I will remember my covenant… I will not reject them… so as to destroy them completely' (vv. 40–44). As James 2:13 puts it, 'Mercy triumphs over judgment.'

Guidelines

Look back over this week's readings.

- Reflect on how the laws of the holiness code contribute to the making of a healthy community. Are there things we can learn from them for our society?
- Do we understand God's rule over us to be as comprehensive as his rule over Israel? Do we keep him locked up in the church or do we allow him to determine our family life, business practices, social policy and attitude towards minorities?

- How might the personal and professional standards required of the priests relate to our church leaders today?
- Having lost touch with the rhythm of the agricultural year in our largely urban world, is there any way we can recapture something of the importance and spiritual significance of an annual round of festivals?
- What do the sabbath principle and the Jubilee year have to teach us about contemporary attitudes to economics, property ownership and dealing with poverty?
- Comparing the summary of the covenant with your own experience, have you known God's blessing when you have lived obediently to him and known his discipline when you have strayed? Can you testify to particular and positive signs of God's blessing on your life? If so, express your thankfulness to him. If you feel his discipline, take note.

FURTHER READING

A.P. Ross, *Holiness to the Lord: A guide to the exposition of the book of Leviticus*, Baker, 2002.

Derek Tidball, *The Message of Leviticus: Free to be holy* (Bible Speaks Today), IVP, 2005.

Gordon Wenham, *The Book of Leviticus*, Eerdmans, 1979.

2 Peter

Preachers sometimes develop old stories or sermons for a new situation. Musicians may adapt an old tune or remix a whole song to produce something different. Using and reworking previous ideas is common practice today.

The second letter of Peter seems to adapt the earlier letter of Jude. Although we cannot be sure, most scholars conclude that Jude was written first, then used and developed by the author of 2 Peter. It was accepted practice in the ancient world to honour other writers by openly borrowing their ideas and then developing them significantly for one's own purposes.

One form of writing valued in the ancient world was the Testament—a farewell speech from the lips of a famous historical figure. Testaments of Solomon, Job, Moses and other patriarchs present the dying hero instructing and exhorting family and friends about how to make the best of their future. The writer of 2 Peter seems to adapt this genre creatively, combining it in a unique way with a pastoral letter.

Testaments are pseudepigraphical—that is, ascribed to someone long dead, who could not actually have written them. A number of recent scholars regard 2 Peter in the same way, as a letter written after Peter's death by an admirer or group of disciples. The authorship of this letter was questioned by some even in the early church because it is more literary and philosophical in style and language than 1 Peter. Silvanus is credited as Peter's secretary in 1 Peter 5:12; could someone else have helped to write 2 Peter? Other sources show that the role of a secretary varied widely, from taking down dictation verbatim to composing an entire letter on behalf of someone else (who would then check it). Perhaps, in the early church, letter writing was a more collaborative process than we tend to assume (see 1 Thessalonians 1:1, where three names are given). I can imagine an elderly Peter producing this letter with help from younger followers—and, for brevity's sake, I shall refer to this group simply as Peter.

While 1 Peter speaks to a church facing pressure and hostility from outside, 2 Peter sees problems arising from within the church. Some Christians are adapting ideas about freedom and desire taken from the culture in which they live, trying to combine these ideas with the gospel of grace.

There are dangers in this approach, which this letter seeks to address.

Quotations are taken from the New Revised Standard Version of the Bible.

1 Grace that leads to godliness

2 Peter 1:1–11

Peter does not name those to whom he is writing—perhaps this letter is for a group of churches, as his first one was (1 Peter 1:1)—but he begins by painting an inspiring picture of who they can become in Christ.

First they need to realise how much God has given them. The good news, which they have believed, is a gift of God's abundant grace, enabling them to know God. This God is a giver, willing and able to provide all that they need. In the gospel, God has already given them precious and wonderful promises, through which their lives can be changed. They can even become 'participants in the divine nature' (v. 4), an unusual phrase that suggests God's presence and power in their lives through the work of the Holy Spirit. Not only have they been cleansed of sins, but they have also been called and chosen to be part of God's 'eternal kingdom', another awesome gift 'richly provided for you' by this God who loves to give (v. 11).

Those who receive this marvellous grace will want to respond appropriately. They are called to 'godliness', a distinctive term that crops up repeatedly in this letter (1:3, 6–7; 2:9; 3:11), along with its opposite, 'ungodly/godless' (2:5–6; 3:7). Peter spells out what godliness looks like in a rich list of qualities and attitudes, which reaches its peak in the deceptive simplicity of the final word, 'love' (agape, 1:5–7). This list might remind us of Paul's 'fruit of the Spirit' (Galatians 5:22–23), and Peter also uses the image of 'fruitfulness' here (v. 8). Cooperation with God's grace requires eagerness and strenuous effort from God's people (vv. 5, 10), a truth which they forget at their peril (v. 9). They need to choose to live godly lives, drawing on all the resources that God gives.

One religious mentality, still common today, says that we have to be good in order to please God and get what we want from God. The stirring opening verses of 2 Peter remind us of the alternative, gospel view: with God's help, we strive to live good lives as a grateful response to all that God has already done for us and given to us.

2 Remembering wisely

2 Peter 1:12–21

Peter has been telling his readers (or hearers: most would probably hear the letter read aloud) gospel truths that they already know. Yet he feels a need to 'keep on reminding' them, to continually 'refresh [their] memory' (1:12–13). Familiar truths can be forgotten, all the more so when someone else is trying to undermine them with different ideas. Peter sees a need to help Christians remember what really matters. Sensing that his own life is nearly over, he decides to preserve his words in written form in this letter (v. 15).

Personal testimony has always been powerful and persuasive; it challenges, and helps to build faith. As one of only three disciples who witnessed Jesus' transfiguration (Mark 9:1–8), Peter revisits that special memory here (vv. 16–18). Some in the churches have been looking away from Jesus, as we shall see shortly. Peter points them back to the Son of God, whose Lordship was emphatically affirmed by the Father in a vision of radiance and magnificence. This is not just some spiritual fantasy, Peter insists: he was there and it really happened. The teaching of one who actually witnessed the revelation of God in Jesus Christ should be valued above all other.

Peter also urges his hearers to remember past witnesses (vv. 19–21). Perhaps in response to some who are sceptical about prophecy, Peter affirms the value of the Old Testament prophets. These were 'men and women moved by the Holy Spirit', who spoke words from God, and their testimony was confirmed in the words and actions of Jesus (v. 19). Now the teaching of the prophets and of Jesus himself continues to dispel the gloom of this world and to illuminate people's inner ignorance in preparation for Christ's return—which will be even more glorious than his transfiguration. Peter will explore this theme later.

Deciding what is worth keeping and remembering is a challenge for us today, in our information-saturated world. 2 Peter urges us to keep hold of the truths taught by God's faithful witnesses in the Old and New Testaments, and to keep reminding each other of God's good news.

3 False teachers and their judgment

2 Peter 2:1–10a; Jude

Like other New Testament letters, 2 Peter was written in response to particular events and concerns. The agenda hinted at in the opening chapter now becomes clear: false teachers are damaging the churches.

Peter seems to be using the letter of Jude (see Introduction): look out for similarities with 2 Peter (for example, compare verse 4 with Jude 6, verse 10 with Jude 8, and 3:1–3 with Jude 17–18). But notice also the differences: for example, Jude does not mention Noah or Lot, as Peter does (vv. 5–7). Here we see a pastor using an earlier, much valued letter because it speaks to the church of his day, but adapting it to meet the new situation.

Peter contrasts the false teachers with the truthfulness of the prophets and apostles, highlighted in his previous two paragraphs. The new voices arise from within the church and deny the authority of Jesus, 'the Master who bought them' (v. 1). Instead of serving the Lord Jesus, who redeemed them from spiritual slavery, they look away from the cross. Bad theology becomes evident in bad behaviour as they serve their own desires. The details are not spelled out, but lack of self-restraint (particularly in sexual matters) and insatiable desire for wealth are both indicated. These teachers deny that God will ever judge human beings for their actions.

Peter proclaims a God of judgment and mercy. Citing examples from the past (Genesis 6, 7 and 19), he shows that God does judge the wicked and save the godly. Peter follows Jewish traditions found in books such as 1 Enoch (a text quoted in Jude 14–15). Puzzling over Genesis 6:1–4, these traditions interpreted the 'sons of God' as fallen angels or 'Watchers', whose illicit relationships with human women helped to prompt God's judgment in the flood. These angels were understood to be imprisoned by God until the final day of judgment.

Peter believes that God will judge, but also that God saves. Noah and Lot, with their families, provide evidence of this salvation and give encouragement to faithful believers in each generation. Those who follow 'the way of truth', and live it out in right actions, have nothing to fear.

4 Freedom that enslaves

2 Peter 2:10b–22

Peter's warnings about the false teachers continue unabated. Like Jude, he uses a polemical style which may sound harsh and unbalanced to us but would have been more familiar to many of his original hearers. Rhetorical techniques of vilifying opponents and exalting people you admired were used in the ancient world to help mould character, by clarifying vice and virtue.

A vivid picture is painted of the false teachers. Their apparent plausibility, which attracts some church members, is totally undermined by their actions. Uncontrolled sexual desire and greed are mentioned here, as previously, along with arrogance and ignorance, irrationality and dedication to pleasure. Their contempt for 'the glorious ones' (angels, v. 10b) may be part of their denial that God will judge, since angels were expected to implement God's judgment. These heretics entice new and unsteady Christians with the intoxicating promise of 'freedom'—yet, ironically, find themselves enslaved to their own desires and addictions (v. 19). Here are established Christians, part of the church fellowship, who have known the 'way of righteousness' and deliberately turned their back on it (2:13, 20–21; compare Hebrews 6:1–8).

In his response, Peter again looks to the Old Testament. He thinks of Balaam, who tried to use his apparent spiritual powers for financial gain until his own donkey comically rebuked him. Unable to curse God's people, Balaam later tried sexual enticement to lead them into idolatry (Numbers 22—25; 31:16). In his scriptures, Peter finds warnings that speak powerfully to his own day and circumstances.

The identify of the false teachers has puzzled scholars because the letter describes them in fairly general terms. We only have Peter's depiction of them, not their own voices. Some argue that they were Gnostics, but they lack certain elements of Gnostic belief. It is more likely that they picked up ideas from various groups in the culture around them. Among these were the Epicureans, who saw God as distant and rejected ideas of divine judgment, while proclaiming freedom of the will and fulfilment of desire. Then, as now, such views would find a more eager audience than a message of self-control in service of the divine Master.

5 Patience with a purpose

2 Peter 3:1–10

Like many persuasive speakers, Peter briefly recaps on key points from this and his previous letter (presumably 1 Peter). He wants to remind his hearers of the truth taught by the apostles and prophets, and stir them up to continue living by it (vv. 1–2).

The false teachers again come into view, full of sarcasm as they seek to justify their passion for pleasure-seeking. Since God's great judgment, promised by prophets of old, has still not appeared, they mock the whole idea that such a day will ever arrive.

Exploring the theme of judgment, Peter uses vivid imagery of flood and fire, which we need to handle carefully. Fire can totally destroy; it can also be used to melt and purify materials such as precious metals. Peter depicts judgment in these terms, saying, 'The earth and everything that is done on it will be disclosed' (v. 10). Some manuscripts say '… will be burned up', but the word meaning 'discovered' or 'laid bare' is probably the original. God will not destroy his creation but will uncover what people have done. When all is revealed, all human beings will be judged. A renewed creation will then emerge, cleansed of corruption, just as the earth emerged when the waters of the flood subsided in Noah's day.

But if the world is so sinful, why are we still waiting for the final day of judgment? This was an issue in Peter's day, and it remains one in ours. As usual, Peter turns to his scriptures for wisdom, citing the words of Psalm 90:4: a period that seems endless to us is like a mere day from the eternal, divine perspective (v. 8). God will bring judgment, in God's own good time. The Lord will return and catch some people unawares, 'like a thief' who breaks in when some are not on the lookout.

The key issue in all this is patience—not that we are patient with God, but that God is patient with us (v. 9). In these 'last days' between Christ's first coming and his return, God is giving time for more people to repent and be saved. So we should be grateful for the delay, Peter insists, not angry or demoralised. God's patience gives Christians an opportunity, which is spelled out in the verses that follow.

6 Keep growing in grace

2 Peter 3:11–18

The opportunity that we are given by God's patience, Peter declares, is to live well, 'leading lives of holiness and godliness' (v. 11). He has already spelled out what this looks like in the opening section of the letter. His reference to God wanting 'all to come to repentance' (3:9; see Mark 13:10) indicates that spreading the gospel is also part of the godly life to which all Christians are called. There is no hint here of simply sitting back and relaxing until the end comes. Instead, Christians are to 'wait' (the word suggests being actively expectant) and speed the coming day of God, presumably by leading more and more people to repentance and faith. This is the 'salvation' that God's patience brings (v. 15). Christians are to strive for what is good here and now, giving a glimpse in their lives of the 'righteousness' that will come when God cleanses and renews all of creation.

Similar themes crop up in the letters of Paul: Romans 2:1–11 is one example. Perhaps Peter has Paul's teaching in mind, since he now un-expectedly mentions his fellow apostle (v. 15). He commends Paul's wisdom, while conceding that it can be misunderstood and distorted. Perhaps the false teachers were using some choice quotations from Paul, about Christ bringing freedom from the law, to help to justify their behaviour. A careful reading of Paul's letters makes it clear that he rejected such distortions of the gospel of grace that he preached.

Through some of Peter's remarks, we glimpse the development of what we now call 'the Bible'. Peter has already placed the teaching of apostles such as himself alongside the words of the Old Testament pro-phets (1:18–21; 3:1–2). Now he mentions, almost in passing, that Paul's letters carry an authority that puts them on the same level as 'the other scriptures' (v. 16). An agreed canon of inspired and authoritative writings is gradually emerging.

After a final warning, Peter closes on an upbeat note of encouragement. Those who know Jesus Christ can keep growing in grace. So let praise to the Lord and Saviour continue until the final day dawns.

Guidelines

- Do you sometimes forget the things that matter most? Have you been struck by any important spiritual truths in this letter that you needed reminding of, as Peter's audience did?
- Think about Peter's call to keep growing in grace and godliness. Pray through the qualities he lists in 1:5–7. Are you motivated to strive for this kind of holiness by your awareness of all that God has given you, or by the thought of Jesus' return? Or do other motives drive you?
- Peter seems happy to use some ideas from his culture (he adapts current techniques of persuasive speech), yet vehemently rejects others (the Epicurean beliefs embraced by the false teachers). How do we decide what to accept or adapt from our own culture and what to reject? Does Peter's instinct to reflect on scripture help in this decision-making?
- What do you do when you strongly disagree with others in the church? Is it ever appropriate to condemn those you disagree with, as forcefully as 2 Peter does? When and how do we need to speak out strongly?
- How do you feel about the future? Hopeful? Doubtful? Cynical? Impatient? Acknowledge your own feelings. Reflect on the prospect of Jesus' return as Lord and Judge: does that have any effect on how you feel and think about the future? Are you prompted to any action?

FURTHER READING

R.J. Bauckham, *Jude, 2 Peter* (Word Biblical Commentaries), Word, 1983. A detailed and very influential commentary.

G.L. Green, *Jude & 2 Peter* (Baker Exegetical Commentary), Baker, 2008. A detailed and up-to-date commentary.

N.T. Wright, *Early Christian Letters for Everyone*, SPCK, 2011. Brief, to the point and very readable, from a leading scholar.

God's mission, human involvement

Recently I heard a fascinating lecture by Professor Steve Walton of the London School of Theology, exploring the concept of the *Missio Dei* (God's mission) in the light of the Acts of the Apostles.

This concept has grown in prominence over the last few decades and emphasises that the church's task is to discern God's mission and share in it. God has always been involved in his mission, and the church, up to the present day, has been called not to devise its own missions but to join God in the whole breadth of his mission to creation as well as through the gospel.

In summary, Professor Walton was able to show that, in large measure, Acts indicates a deep and broad awareness that the church's mission is given and directed by God. He rightly pointed out, however, that one of the issues this raises for us is the role of humans in the *Missio Dei*. If it is God's plan, inaugurated and enabled by God, what role, if any, do humans have? Are we, as one commentator suggests, reduced to being puppets of the divine?

For the next week, we will explore this issue. What does Acts (specifically, six passages from the first half of Acts) suggest is the balance between the divine and the human involvement in carrying out God's mission and what are the implications for us today?

In working with this focus, we are touching on much wider concerns. On the larger scale, it relates to subjects such as predestination and free will, which, while they no longer divide Christian communities as they did during the Reformation and for centuries afterwards, are never far from us in terms of the extent to which humans are determined by their genes or their social context. On the more personal scale, it flows into Christian practices such as prayer and discerning God's will.

1 Keeping going

Acts 1:15–26

The picture painted in Acts suggests that the apostles and the church often took a much more initiatory and active role in their decisions and the shaping of their lives than the term *Missio Dei* might imply to some.

One example would be the decision to select a new 'twelfth apostle' to replace Judas. The text gives no indication that the apostles received a directive from Jesus to do this or that the Holy Spirit in any way changed things so that they felt they had to do it. The process was explained by Peter to the church, and then we are told, 'So they proposed two' (v. 23) and Matthias was chosen by lot.

This episode shows us a process that is intended to conform to the discerned will of God. The proposal was made in the context of a most prayerful community, the rationale for replacing Judas was scripturally warranted, and the church asked God to show them 'which one of these two *you have chosen*' (v. 24, emphasis added). Casting lots was not understood as a lottery but as a way of creating space for God's will to be manifested to them. However, this method for making the choice was, in itself, as far as the text indicates, a human one: there is nothing to suggest that the apostles were directed by God toward this *modus operandi*.

The words 'One of these must become a witness with us to his resurrection' (v. 22) are worth noting. Here, the 'must' is to be understood as a divine necessity: Peter is saying, in effect, that this is what God's will and purposes require. However, the arrival at this decision comes through the human understanding of scripture, and certainly the selection of the two men to be 'proposed' seems to have involved some apostolic consultation rather than a divine searchlight. So here we have a complex picture of the interplay of the divine and the human: the church seeks God's will through scripture; in addition, through prayer, the community remains open to, desirous of and responsive to God's will. God does not compel any of this, but it stems from the desire of the community to live out his will. Human freedom is not being repressed.

2 The Day of Pentecost

Acts 2:1–41

One critique of yesterday's passage from Acts 1 is that the procedure used by the apostles to select their twelfth member only serves to illustrate the difference between life before and life after Pentecost. Clearly, what happens at Pentecost is vital for us, but I am not convinced that we can dismiss the episode as irrelevant on the grounds that we now live after Pentecost.

On the Day of Pentecost, when the Spirit promised by Jesus comes to the disciples, it does seem that the focus is on God's initiative. From the 'sound like the rush of a violent wind' to the tongues of fire that 'rested on each of them' (vv. 2–3), it appears that the disciples had no choice in the matter. The point that Peter emphasises in his explanation, especially in his quotation from the prophet Joel, is that God's Spirit is given to all, irrespective of age, gender or status: the tongues did not rest only on the twelve apostles but on all 120 of the gathered assembly. Then there is the outcome from the filling with the Spirit: they 'began to speak in other languages, as the Spirit gave them ability' (v. 4). Again, this implies that they had no choice in the matter, although it could mean that everyone was enabled to speak, not necessarily made to speak, in these languages.

There are other features that we can note to gain a better sense of proportion about the divine initiative and human participation involved. For instance, Luke has emphasised the willingness of the disciples to wait for the promised gift and, indeed, their willingness to cooperate with God through their devotion to prayer (1:14). Equally significant is Peter's claim, 'Then everyone who calls on the name of the Lord shall be saved' (2:21). His command, 'Be baptised every one of you…' is in response to his hearers' enquiry (vv. 37–38), and the passage climaxes in Luke's statement, 'Those who welcomed his message were baptised' (v. 41). 'Welcomed' suggests a free human response.

So we see again a rather subtle balance between God's inbreaking power and human freedoms.

3 An awesome event

Acts 5:1–11

This is, for many of us, one of the most troublesome stories in Acts. Here we have two believers who are struck down by God himself, apparently for being only very generous and not totally so. The incident recalls Paul's words in 1 Corinthians that if we eat and drink at the Lord's Supper 'in an unworthy manner', we can expect, at the very least, to become ill and maybe even to die (1 Corinthians 11:27–30).

The preceding verses (4:32–37) provide the context for this story. Many of the Christian community chose to sell their possessions and shared the proceeds with any in need. Ananias and his wife Sapphira followed suit—apparently. They sold their property but, before handing the money over to the apostles, they kept some of it back for themselves.

Confronted by Peter, neither Ananias nor his wife will admit their wrongdoing and so they fall down dead. The text stops short of saying that this is a divine punishment, although that is probably the intention of the text. We could, of course, argue that this story developed after the event—that is, that the two disciples fell dead inexplicably and so (perhaps to avoid the impression that it was dangerous to sell up and turn over your wealth to the apostles—after all, maintaining your land was a divine responsibility: see 1 Kings 21), the story of their deceit was told to account for their sudden deaths. However, we are given no warrant for reading it in this way. Does disobedience to God lead to death?

Actually, though, this is not the whole story. First, the decision to sell up was a voluntary one. Peter emphasises that, even after he had sold the property, the ownership of the money was with Ananias (v. 4). So Acts 4:34 does not mean that people were compelled to sell up, or that everyone did so. Nor was it a sin to sell one's birthright and profit from it rather than investing it in the new people of God. Again, the disciples did not have to sell *everything*: Barnabas does not appear to have done so, and he is presented as a model to be emulated (4:37). The sin of Ananias and Sapphira was that of letting Satan 'fill their hearts' and lying to the Holy Spirit (v. 3), and then, when an opportunity for repentance was offered, failing to respond (v. 4). So, human cooperation, not compulsion, is being emphasised in this story.

4 Restructuring

Acts 6:1–7

God's mission is moving on apace. Verse 1 not only tells us that 'the disciples were increasing in number' but also indicates that the response to the gospel was becoming ever more varied, with Hellenists as well as Hebrews joining the church. It shows, too, that the church was seeking to meet the social needs of the widows. Care of widows was enjoined in the law (Deuteronomy 24:17–21), and, unlike the Pharisees who 'devoured widows' houses' (Luke 20:47), the early church was committed to helping them. This 'social care' is part of God's mission.

We are not told how the church discerned that such compassion was part of God's mission, but the criteria for selecting the seven helpers strongly support the view that the church saw it as such, and were committed to participating in it. The people selected needed to be 'full of the Spirit and of wisdom' (v. 3). The words 'full of the Spirit' indicate that they would be involved in God's mission as generated by the Spirit, and the reference to wisdom may reflect Luke's earlier descriptions of Jesus (see Luke 2:40, 52). The fact that these people would be appointed to the task by the apostles endorses this understanding: it was not a necessary but ultimately divisive role for the church, but something requiring full apostolic endorsement.

For our purposes, it is important to note that the selection of the seven helpers is not presented as a move dictated by God or even founded on the apostles' understanding of the Old Testament scriptures. It is presented as the apostles' solution to a dilemma, not a divine directive, and the whole community was involved: 'What they said pleased the whole community, and they chose…' (v. 5). So, not only did the community help to discern the rightness of the apostolic proposal; they actually chose the seven men.

We are told that this move furthered the mission of God. The 'word of God' (presumably the gospel message) continued to spread, and the numbers 'in Jerusalem' continued to expand and diversify. It is surely significant that 'a great many of the priests became obedient to the faith' (v. 7).

5 Philip and the Ethiopian

Here is a passage that, at first reading, emphasises the divine initiative. Philip leaves his successful, if somewhat erratic, evangelistic mission in Samaria to travel to a wilderness road at the behest of an angel (v. 26). Angels, especially in Luke's writings, are potent divine messengers, as we see in the birth narratives (see, for example, Luke 1:5–20). They are not to be disobeyed, they come with compelling messages from God and any trifling with them (as in Zachariah's case) can bring dire consequences. So, perhaps we are being told that Philip had no choice: he just had to obey. Furthermore, when he spots the Ethiopian's chariot (probably slow-moving because it would have been drawn by an ox), he is told by the Holy Spirit, 'Go over to this chariot and join it' (v. 29). The story ends with another compelling divine intervention: 'The Spirit of the Lord snatched Philip away… Philip found himself at Azotus' (vv. 39–40).

Nevertheless, the account also indicates that there is plenty of room for humans, attuned to God's purposes, to act as independent but co-operative people. Philip runs to the chariot, hears the Ethiopian reading and asks a seemingly non-directive question: 'Do you understand what you are reading?' (v. 30). This leads the Ethiopian to extend an invitation to Philip to join him in the chariot, and a fairly normal conversation ('normal', that is, given the circumstances and the subject) is reported.

The Ethiopian hears the gospel and, seeing water, asks if he is allowed to be baptised. There is no command from Philip (as there was from Peter on the Day of Pentecost: Acts 2:38). Rather, the Ethiopian initiates the process of his acceptance into the Christian community.

Certainly, as in many other 'breakthrough' situations (for example, the extension of the gospel to Gentiles in Acts 10), Luke makes it absolutely clear that God has taken the initiative in this episode. This is not a case of the evangelist pushing beyond God's boundaries; rather, Philip follows God's lead. However, Luke in no way minimises human free participation in God's will or implies that human discernment and initiative are not required.

6 Saul's conversion

This very well-known, highly influential and significant event offers one of the strongest cases for the view that God takes all the initiative in running his mission and that humans have little, if any, freedom in the process. God acts; humans obey.

Saul, on setting out for Damascus, intended to destroy the heretical sect of those who followed a supposed 'Messiah', but his firm and humanly authorised intention was totally reversed by direct divine intervention: 'a light from heaven flashed around him' (v. 3). Surely it does not get more compelling than the inbreaking of God's *shekinah* glory? Yet it does, for then Saul hears a divine voice, and a miraculous sign occurs as he is blinded (compare Zachariah's experience, Luke 1:20).

Equally strong evidence for the sense of divine compulsion is provided by the experience of Ananias, the bit player in this remarkable drama: 'The Lord said to him in a vision…' (v. 10). This voice issues several commands: 'Get up and go… Look for… Go…'. Ananias does exactly what he has been told and the events unfold just as the divine voice has directed. This voice is the voice of God: 'the Lord' is repeated many times. Furthermore, the message given to Ananias adds to the sense of divine compulsion: Saul is described as *'an instrument* whom *I have chosen*… I myself will show him how much he *must* suffer' (vv. 15–16, emphasis added).

Even in this pivotal event, however, divine compulsion is not the whole story. First, Ananias says, 'Here I am, Lord' (v. 10). These words may recall the response of the young Samuel (1 Samuel 3:10), but they certainly indicate Ananias' choice to make himself available for God. Unlike Samuel, he seems to be able to recognise the Lord's voice without any trouble. His familiarity with God is portrayed in the conversation that ensues: he seems to speak quite comfortably about his own perspective, including his anxieties about meeting Saul, and God does not strike him dead! God is looking for a willing partner in his mission, even at this critical juncture. Throughout this part of Saul's conversion experience, the free participation of the human agent is vital.

Guidelines

Through this selection of passages from Acts, we have been exploring the interconnectedness of divine initiative and human response and responsibility in the developing mission of the early church. One important challenge for us, if we wish to cooperate with God in his mission, is about how we can discern God's will. In our readings over the past week, we can see all kinds of ways in which the early church seems to have done this. Reread the passages and note as many different methods as you can. How do they compare with your own practices?

What place does prayer play in discerning God's will? Have you ever had the kind of conversation with God that Ananias (or Abraham) had (see Acts 9:10–16; Genesis 18:23–32)? If so, what was the outcome? Did you understand God better; were you enabled to carry out his will more faithfully; did you have a clearer sense that God was with you; did God reject your approaches and questions? When might it be appropriate to engage God in this kind of way?

If you are interested in pursuing this theme further, the following passages may be helpful:

- Acts 10:1–20, 44–48
- Acts 11:22–30
- Acts 15:22–35
- Acts 16:6–10
- Acts 21:5–14, 17–26
- Acts 23:12–24
- Acts 27:9–26

Wisdom for life

Wisdom plays a larger role in the Bible than first meets the eye. Most obvious, due to their extensive use of 'wisdom' terminology, are three Old Testament books—Proverbs, Job and Ecclesiastes. Song of Songs often gets bundled with them, not least because of its association with Solomon. In addition, many scholars hold that some of the psalms should be classified as 'wisdom' psalms. Psalms 1, 34 and 73, for example, contain material that resonates with the book of Proverbs. Then, some of the stories in the Old Testament portray what the life of 'wisdom' looks like in men and women such as Joseph, Daniel and Esther.

Beyond these instances, Old Testament wisdom is rooted in the drama of the whole biblical story—both in looking backward to creation and in looking forward to Christ. Looking backwards, God is portrayed in wisdom literature as the Creator of the world. Proverbs 8 describes God as the builder of creation, who used wisdom to make the world (vv. 22–31). Elsewhere, Proverbs refers to the created world and the lessons to be learnt from it (for example, 6:6–8; 30:18–19, 24–28), as do other parts of wisdom literature (see Job 38—39; Ecclesiastes 1:5–7; 10:20).

From a whole-Bible perspective, wisdom literature also anticipates Christ. In several cases, New Testament writers link 'wisdom' and Jesus. The opening of John's Gospel, for instance, assigns to the *logos* (the 'Word') some of the attributes of wisdom highlighted in Proverbs 8—describing the *logos* in personalised terms, as existing with God before all things and as being God's agent in creation. Then, in 1 Corinthians 1—2, Paul writes about the wisdom of the cross confounding the wisdom of the world, and about Christ as the 'wisdom of God' (for example, 1:24, 30). Elsewhere in his letters (see Philippians 2:5–11; Colossians 1:15–20), Paul arguably uses wisdom theology to show that all the blessings of God's wisdom are now mediated through Jesus, the wisdom of God.

Thus, as we explore the biblical wisdom literature over the next fortnight, we may do so with the confidence that it will provide a way of orienting our everyday lives to creation and to Christ.

Unless otherwise indicated, quotations are taken from the New International Version of the Bible.

1 Biblical wisdom: its Solomon connection

1 Kings 3

If the law is associated with Moses and the Psalms are connected with David, the wisdom literature is most closely linked with the name of Solomon. Jesus himself notes that Solomon was renowned for his wisdom (Matthew 12:42), and the emphasis on Solomon in the biblical wisdom books, particularly Proverbs, is a strong reflection of the tradition about his wisdom.

Intriguingly, the portrayal of Solomon found at the beginning of 1 Kings 3 is somewhat mixed. He builds a temple for the Lord, yet marries outside the covenant (v. 1); he shows his love for the Lord, yet worships at the 'high places' (v. 3). It is a sign of God's great grace, then, that he appears to Solomon in a dream and invites him to ask for anything he wants. There are many things a king might request, given the opportunity to do so: good health and long life, numerous descendants, prosperity for himself and his people, the subjugation of enemies. Yet, in his long response (vv. 6–9), Solomon asks for 'a discerning heart' in order rightly to govern the nation, making it clear (twice in verses 8–9) that they are God's own people.

The Lord is pleased with Solomon's response (v. 10) and promises to give not only the wisdom he has requested—in which he will be without equal—but riches and honour in addition (vv. 11–13). God also promises Solomon long life, but with a condition attached: '*if* you walk in obedience to me' (v. 14). It is perhaps significant that Solomon then leaves Gibeon, chief among the 'high places', and returns to Jerusalem to worship (v. 15).

His wisdom is immediately put to the test by two mothers who claim the same child as their own (vv. 16–28). Solomon's handling of this situation is seen as a demonstration of the gift given to him, as the people 'saw that he had wisdom from God to administer justice' (v. 28). What follows in 1 Kings 4 is a description of how Solomon administered the kingdom (vv. 1–28), once more underscoring wisdom as the source of his governance and widespread fame (vv. 29–34).

In the light of such a beginning, Solomon's ultimate failure, summarised in 1 Kings 11:1–13, is all the more tragic. It not only reminds us of the danger of not living up to our calling, but also leaves us looking for something better, for 'one greater than Solomon' (Matthew 12:42).

2 Biblical wisdom: its cultural background

Proverbs 22:17–29

Although God gave Solomon wisdom, which was immediately demonstrated in his dealings with the two mothers, Solomon revelled in developing the gift he had been given. 1 Kings 4:29–34 describes how he became a student of both the natural creation and neighbouring cultures. The comparison of his wisdom to that of renowned wise figures beyond the borders of Israel implicitly pays tribute to the value of the wisdom of surrounding nations, even while claiming that Solomon's surpassed it.

Much of the surviving wisdom material from ancient Near Eastern societies comes from Egypt. The best-known example is the 'Instruction of Amenemope', which predates Solomon by about 100 years but bears a striking similarity, in structure and content, to the 'Sayings of the wise' section in Proverbs 22:17—24:22. The Egyptian document is divided into 30 sayings (compare Proverbs 22:20) in which Amenemope instructs his son about not robbing the poor (see 22:22), not wearing oneself out in order to get rich (23:4–5), and not moving ancient landmarks (22:28; 23:10–11), among other topics.

Scholars debate whether the biblical authors 'borrowed' the Egyptian material or whether both texts are part of a wider tradition which was happy to appropriate and adapt proven insights about life. Even so, the places where the traditions differ are just as significant. Israel was unique among the nations in seeing one God as creator and ruler of all. Moreover, the king in Israel was understood to rule on behalf of God, rather than having divine status himself. In addition, as we shall see in a subsequent note, Israel's wisdom tradition begins with 'the fear of the Lord' (Proverbs 1:7), implying covenant relationship with God.

This being the case, however, the level of openness towards the wisdom of surrounding nations is even more remarkable. The questions and issues being faced by the people of Israel were the same questions and issues being faced by their pagan neighbours. As the quest for answers to the conundrums of life still continues in the present, we may suspect that growth in wisdom will come not just through the study of God's word but also through ongoing engagement with the surrounding world.

3 Biblical wisdom: its life setting

Proverbs 4

Like its neighbours in the ancient Near East, Israel may have had schools attached to the royal court for the professional development of the nation's leaders. It would perhaps make sense for wisdom literature to have its origins in such formal educational settings. However, an increasing number of scholars suggest that the book of Proverbs can be understood just as readily in the context of the home, with its roots in the everyday insights of 'ordinary' people in both rural and urban settings.

It is certainly clear that Proverbs 1—9 contain the repeated appeal of a 'father' to a 'son' (seen, for example, throughout today's reading), which earths the instruction in a relationship of some kind. The 'father–son' language could be metaphorical for a teacher–pupil relationship or it could represent a genuine family relationship, not least because a 'mother' is also mentioned (1:8; 6:20; 30:17; 31:1–9, 26), which is unusual compared with wisdom documents in other cultures of the time. From the very beginning of their existence, the people of God were called to pass on the faith to subsequent generations. The book of Proverbs may reflect the fact that such education largely took place in the family unit.

This being the case, it should come as no surprise that Christian thinkers have made much of the educational thrust of wisdom literature. The invitation to learn arises out of relationship, and a personal appeal is issued to listen to the parents' instruction (for example, vv. 1, 10, 20). The means by which moral instruction is passed on is multifaceted, comprising a mixture of descriptions, incentives, commands, motivations, illustrations and consequences. It becomes clear from the book of Proverbs as a whole that the 'curriculum' encompasses the appropriate use of speech, respect for others, integrity in relationships, the ability to resolve disputes, the art of discernment, the proper use of wealth and much more. The 'students', for their part, are called on to listen attentively, respond obediently and assimilate carefully what is taught into their lives, where the goal is the formation of moral character. As we shall see next, the larger context of all this, for both parent and child, is a deep reverence for the covenant Lord.

4 Biblical wisdom: its fundamental orientation

Proverbs 1:1–7

Proverbs 1:1–7 effectively forms the foreword to the book, providing its title, purpose and central motif. The title (v. 1) connects the book to Solomon, even though it is clear from elsewhere that other hands contributed to the final collection. The purpose (vv. 2–6), for its readers, has to do with the acquisition of knowledge and wisdom through listening to instruction—leading to understanding, prudent behaviour, justice and fairness. A related goal appears to be the ability to interpret different forms of wisdom material (vv. 2b, 6).

Verse 7 then provides something of a theological principle, the fundamental orientation of wisdom literature—'the fear of the Lord'. This runs as a motif through the wisdom literature (Proverbs 9:10; 31:30; Job 28:28; Ecclesiastes 5:7; 12:13–14). The word 'fear' can connote a sense of terror or dread, while 'respect' may be too weak; the English words 'awe' or 'reverence' perhaps come closest to what is implied in most biblical uses of the word. At the very least, it implies relationship with and dependence on God for wisdom, rather than being wise in one's own eyes (Proverbs 3:7).

The word 'beginning' (v. 7a) carries the sense of 'first' and 'foundation'. If wisdom literature is concerned with living wisely in God's world, then fear of the Lord is the first principle of such a life. Wisdom does not begin in human autonomy but in deep reverence for the Lord God; wisdom is not merely intellectual capacity but is linked with discipline and discernment, shrewdness and skill; wisdom produces a certain kind of character and demonstrates itself in particular sorts of actions.

Incidentally, the fact that 'the Lord' here is 'Yahweh', the special covenant name for God, shows us that wisdom might not be as far removed from other traditions in scripture as has sometimes been thought. Indeed, the notion of 'the fear of the Lord' is rooted in accounts of the exodus from Egypt, the crossing of the Red Sea and the giving of the law (Exodus 14:31; 20:20; Deuteronomy 10:12). The 'fear of the Lord' as an appropriate response to the extraordinary events of salvation is worked out in wisdom literature in a way that also embraces the 'ordinariness' of everyday life.

5 Biblical wisdom: its all-inclusive challenge

Proverbs 9

The book of Proverbs divides into three major parts: chapters 1—9, 10—29 and 30–31. After the prologue (1:1–7) comes a collection of poems in Proverbs 1—9 in which a 'son' is called on to follow the advice of his parents. Drawing on the metaphors of two ways, two houses and two women, the young man is required to choose, as he sets out on the journey of life, between wisdom and folly.

Representing two ways to live, wisdom and folly are portrayed as women calling out to all who will listen (men and women alike) to walk in their ways and to live in their houses (1:20–33; 2:12–19; 4:4–9; 7:6–27; 8:1–36; 9:1–6, 13–18). It is perhaps significant that they call out in public places, where the hustle and bustle of life takes place, reminding us that wisdom embraces not just private concerns but also social activities connected with family, work and community. Proverbs 1—9 thus instructs its readers about the nature of wisdom, providing a lens through which later chapters are to be understood.

Proverbs 10—29 is largely a collection of individual proverbial sayings of the sort most often associated with the book. It is sometimes tempting to reorder these sayings, to gather them into distinct themes. This, however, could obscure the point that their very randomness makes them especially suitable when reflecting on the way we are often required to negotiate what it means to live wisely in the particularities of daily life.

The final section of the book, Proverbs 30—31, moves from short individual sayings to longer poems from Agur (30:1) and Lemuel (31:1).

Crucially, the notion of the 'fear of the Lord' (introduced in 1:7) recurs in all three sections (for example, 1:29; 8:13; 10:27; 14:27; 19:23; 23:17; 31:30). In particular, its placement at the beginning (1:7) and the end (31:30), as well as in 9:10 at the transition from chapters 1—9 to the rest of the book, provides good reason for seeing the whole composition as a unity, as well as a helpful prism for reading its different sections.

6 Biblical wisdom: its holistic worldview

Proverbs 12

Our readings so far should allow us to begin to piece together some facets of the worldview of wisdom literature. For instance, it assumes that God stands behind the making of the world, and that wisdom is necessary for living in his world. Then, beyond the assumption of a created order is the assumption of a moral order. Many individual proverbs, for instance, including some in chapter 12, provide observations on the character of people and the consequences of their actions in terms of a cause–effect sequence.

While some of these insights might be apparent from empirical, common-sense observation of the world, we must not forget that wisdom literature begins with the fear of the Lord as the beginning of wisdom (Proverbs 1:7). This suggests a model which understands that we shouldn't necessarily observe the 'world' first, and then see how it might square with scripture; rather, we view the world through lenses informed by scripture, understood through a fear of the Lord that shapes our head, heart and hands.

When we do this, it becomes clear that one of the most profound points about the worldview of wisdom literature is that it is intensely concerned with ordinary, everyday life. Wisdom literature should lay to rest, once and for all, any notion that getting on with the day-by-day routine of living in the world has nothing to do with serving God. The distinctions we can be so prone to making in our lives between the 'sacred' and the 'secular' would have meant very little to those behind the wisdom literature of Israel. Take, for example, the range of topics treated in Proverbs 12, embracing marriage (v. 4), speech (vv. 6, 12–13), care for animals (v. 10), work (vv. 11, 24), receiving insults (v. 16), honesty (v.

19), and friends (v. 26). Wisdom literature is concerned with the whole of life and its various dimensions. The very practical matters of how I do my job, speak about others, bring up my children, conduct my finances and treat my spouse have to do with my fear of the Lord.

Here, then, is an encouragement that God gives wisdom to guide his people through the delights and demands of everyday life.

Guidelines

Taking the fear of the Lord as its foundation, wisdom in the Bible encompasses a range of ideas related to insight and understanding, as well as moral and resourceful ways of behaving. Wisdom is a way of thinking—and living—that results in harmony with God and with others in every arena of life. It is grounded in the orderly regulation of the world by the Creator God. Wisdom is not, therefore, a 'secular' alternative to other, more 'sacred' parts of the Bible. Nor should it come as a surprise that Israel was able to engage with surrounding cultures, gleaning insight where those cultures reflected God's truth, because of the recognition that he is the source of all wisdom.

- How do you react to the phrase 'the fear of the Lord'? How does it help you to understand the wisdom of God in everyday life?
- What questions and issues of life do you share with your neighbours in the world that surrounds you? How can you apply biblical wisdom to those issues?
- Where do you see opportunities to learn and to teach wisdom within your own everyday contexts: at work, at home or in the community?

10–16 June

1 A wisdom that builds

Proverbs 3

It sometimes comes as a surprise for readers of scripture to learn that the book of Proverbs hardly ever refers to major themes of the Bible such as covenant, redemption, law, kingship and temple. Of course, given that 'the fear of the Lord' is the first principle of wisdom, it could be said that the sayings everywhere presuppose the special saving relationship established between 'the Lord' (Yahweh, God's covenant name) and his people.

As it turns out, however, wisdom is rooted even further back—in creation—and grounded in God's providence. Wisdom is equated with the tree of life in verse 18, echoing the early chapters of Genesis. Through wisdom God founded the world (vv. 19–20; see 8:22–31). In using the verbs 'laid' and 'set in place', Proverbs 3:19 portrays God as an architect and builder who establishes a strong foundation and secures in place a building's walls or columns. God constructs this cosmic house by his wisdom, understanding and knowledge (vv. 19–20). Incidentally, these are the same sort of qualities possessed by those involved in the building of the tabernacle (Exodus 31:1–3; 35:30—36:7) and the temple (1 Kings 7:14), both structures being microcosms of God's creation, built with wisdom, understanding and knowledge.

Proverbs 24:3–4, using the same words, reminds us that we too build in harmony with God's own work, in God's own way. The wisdom used by God in building and sustaining the house of creation is the same wisdom now given to his people, to be eagerly desired by his people, in order to live wisely in his world.

As the rest of the book demonstrates, the call to wisdom is applicable in different spheres of life—at the city gates and in the market squares, in our homes and in our workplaces, in our bedrooms and in our boardrooms—where God's people are called to wise 'building' in God's house of creation. Far from being removed from the rhythms of our everyday life, such 'building' embraces a range of skills and practices, worked out concretely in the kitchen, on the field and at the desk, wherever God has called us, and where the model for such activities is God's own wise work.

2 A wisdom that observes

Proverbs 6

Solomon, internationally famed for his wisdom, composer of thousands of proverbs and songs, was also a student of the natural sciences. In line with the original mandate given by the Creator God to human beings, Solomon's wisdom incorporated an accumulation of insights from the natural world, his proverbs speaking about 'plant life, from the cedar of Lebanon to the hyssop that grows out of walls', and 'about animals and birds, reptiles and fish' (1 Kings 4:33).

This grounding of the wisdom tradition in creation is seen in the book of Proverbs itself, where the acquisition of sagacity involves not just the careful observation of daily life, consideration of personal experience and rumination on the know-how of others passed down through the ages, but also reflection on the created world.

Within this wider perspective, on two occasions the wise teacher draws attention to the industriousness of one of the smallest creatures on the face of the earth—the ant (vv. 6–11; 30:24–25). In this case, the lesson is for the lazy person, who is called to 'go... consider... and be wise'. The sequence is important: 'go' (shake off your inactivity), 'consider' (observe, reflect on and learn from the ant's diligence), and 'be wise' (internalise the lesson and make it habitual in your own life). Parents and teachers might like to note that the description of the ant's commendable behaviour and the three imperatives are combined with rhetorical questions—'How long will you lie there, you sluggard? When will you get up from your sleep?' (v. 9)—along with a warning: 'poverty will come on you like a bandit and scarcity like an armed man' (v. 11). Description, commands, questions and warning—with some gentle mocking—are all artfully blended together in a concern for the welfare of the community as a whole.

Centuries later, one greater than Solomon called on his listeners to 'look at the birds of the air' and 'see how the lilies of the field grow' (Matthew 6:26–30). Such wisdom, far from being a special source of knowledge for the select few, is still available to all who have eyes to see.

3 A wisdom that evaluates

Proverbs need to be used fittingly, with an appropriate application for different circumstances. Proverbs 26:3 seems to recognise this in describing what is required in order to give direction to a horse and a donkey: what works in one case may not work for the other. The need to evaluate a fitting application becomes clear when individual proverbs appear to recommend different courses of action, as in verses 4–5. Even some rabbis struggled with the 'contradiction' between these two sayings, deciding that the fool should be corrected only when interpretion of the Torah was at stake.

As it happens, the seemingly random mixture of individual proverbs throughout the book means that the sayings would work on their own if they were isolated from each other; placed side by side, however, they do something more. As the second line in each case indicates, there is wisdom in both courses of action. On the one hand, in responding like a fool, we risk becoming like the fool. On the other hand, it's not always wise to let fools have the last word, in case they mistake their folly for wisdom. All of this is even more significant when there are others around, listening in—during a team meeting, a presentation or a coffee break conversation. On their own, the pair of proverbs say nothing about what sort of circumstances require which type of response, or even how the 'fool' should be identified. The point is that, at such and such a time, one response is to be favoured over the other. Wisdom, in this case, is a matter of what is fitting and what is timely—knowing what to say and when to say it.

The two aphorisms also provide a helpful pointer to the way proverbial sayings work more generally. Implicit in the book of Proverbs is the call to live with the ambiguities of life, often in relationship with others, and to navigate wisely through alternative courses of action. In such situations, individual proverbs are not moral absolutes that apply in all circumstances; no one saying contains the whole truth on a particular matter. The application requires discernment—careful reading of the proverb itself *and* the situation in which we find ourselves.

4 A wisdom that prays

Apart from what we glean from the sayings in Proverbs 30, we know nothing of their author, Agur son of Jakeh (v. 1). But he bequeathes to us the only prayer in the book (vv. 7–9): a twofold request describing how he wants to live before he dies. First of all, having declared that God's own word is 'flawless' (v. 5), he expresses a desire to be a man of truth and integrity: 'Keep falsehood and lies far from me' (v. 8).

His second request also begins with a negative petition ('give me neither poverty nor riches'), which is then expanded positively: 'but give me only my daily bread'. The prayer goes on to muse that life at either extreme of the socio-economic spectrum might lead to faithlessness. The self-sufficiency that results from wealth might lead to a denial of the Lord. The insufficiency that results from poverty might lead to crime, profaning God's name in the process.

It's easy to see why the Bible has been claimed to be on the side of both the rich and the poor. The sheer breadth of its teaching on riches means that a wealthy Abraham or Job over there can be set against the warnings of Amos or the letter of James over here. The book of Proverbs itself recognises that money brings undeniable advantages even while it also carries inevitable drawbacks. Proverbs encourages neither prosperity nor austerity; it allows us neither to idolise a life of luxury nor to idealise a 'simple life'.

Agur's 'just enough' principle is reiterated in different ways throughout scripture. His request calls to mind God's provision of manna in the wilderness (Exodus 16), sufficient for the needs of the day, and it reaches forward to the petition for 'daily bread' in the Lord's prayer (Matthew 6:11). Raising financial help for those suffering a famine, Paul calls on churches to give generously of their 'plenty' so that others who are hard pressed might be relieved (2 Corinthians 8:13–15).

Agur's prayer also provides a model for Christians today. Alongside an awareness of his own weakness is a recognition of God's power to make people poor or rich, a concern about the consequences of sin and a desire to stay faithful above all else. That much, at least, we know about this ancient follower of the Lord.

5 A wisdom that works

Several scholars argue that the composer of this passage is drawing on motifs from so-called 'heroic' poetry, which described the mighty deeds of warriors or heroes. Verse 10, in the NIV, calls the woman 'a wife of noble character' (see also v. 29); it could be translated as 'a woman of strength' or '… excellence', but the word can also carry military connotations, suggesting that she is to be understood as 'a valiant woman' or 'a woman of valour'. The woman's activities are thus celebrated in heroic terms. Here is a composition akin to a heroic poem about someone engaged in everyday labour; so far as we know, there is nothing else like it in the ancient world.

Significantly, then, we reach the end of the book of Proverbs and discover that the model to emulate is not a religious 'professional', like a priest or a prophet or a scribe, but a woman whose faith is shown in her daily life. In fact, this remarkable portrayal is the Bible's fullest description of the regular activity of an 'ordinary' person—a woman who 'fears the Lord' (v. 30), whose wisdom is demonstrated in her everyday activities of being a wife to her husband and a mother to her children, providing for her family, managing her household, engaging in international trade in cloths and textiles, negotiating the purchase of fields, looking out for the poor, and more besides!

Furthermore, in a book that begins by portraying wisdom as a woman inviting people to come to her to receive insight and understanding from God, the woman of Proverbs 31:10–31 is arguably a picture of wisdom itself—and so is applicable to men as much as to women. It applies to all because it sets out the ideal of practical wisdom, involving words and deeds, operating in every sphere of life—at home, in the fields, at the city gate, in the market square—embracing the daily rhythms of eating, drinking, working, sleeping.

Here is someone who supremely embodies what Proverbs says about wisdom. The book that begins with 'the fear of the Lord' as 'the beginning of wisdom' (1:7) concludes with a demonstration of what it means to fear the Lord in everyday life.

6 A wisdom that questions

Ecclesiastes 1; Job 31

On the face it, the book of Proverbs appears to be full of confident as-
sertions about life and the consequences of living a certain way. On its
own, it might give the impression that every question about existence
can be answered, every puzzle solved, every doubt removed. Ecclesiastes
and Job belong to the same wisdom tradition, however, and they tell a
different story!

Ecclesiastes relates the struggles of a Solomon-like figure (perhaps
Solomon himself) who had wisdom and wealth and power, yet found
himself in an existential crisis where life seemed empty and enigmatic.
He set out to explore every dimension of existence 'under the sun', but
no matter what area he examined or threw himself into, the conclusion
was always the same: 'meaningless' (vv. 2, 14), literally 'vaporous', like a
mist, here today and gone tomorrow. If a resolution of any kind is present in the book, it's found in the closing verses, which come back to the
starting point of wisdom—the fear of the Lord (12:13–14). Along the
way, we read of the author's struggle, and might well sympathise if we
have struggled in similar ways.

Likewise, the book of Job provides a counterpoint to the seeming
confidence of Proverbs. Job's sympathisers draw on conventional wisdom
that God will bless those who are good and judge those who do evil.
On this basis, they conclude that Job is suffering because he has done
something wrong, whereas Job insists he hasn't. Job himself believes in
the principle of retribution, but that's precisely his dilemma: his suffering
has turned his worldview upside down. God, he thinks, has become his
enemy, and he calls on God to answer these charges against him.

As it turns out, the significance of the book is not in what it says
about suffering but in what it teaches about relationship with God. It is
the quality of Job's relationship with God that is at stake in the opening
conversations between God and Satan (Job 1—2); and the book ends not
with understanding on Job's part but with repentance as Job retreats from
any insistence that he is owed an answer (42:1–6).

Biblical wisdom, then, requires all these different voices in order to
reflect on the range and richness of human experience in God's world.

Guidelines

Some people make a habit of reading a chapter of the book of Proverbs every day, one for every day of the month. Without a doubt, such a practice could turn out to be helpfully formative. At a time when spirituality is seen to be about self-awareness and self-discovery, something that benefits me as a self-actualised individual, the book of Proverbs reminds us that spiritual formation doesn't float free from our ongoing relationship with the Lord God or with other people. Nor will our spirituality develop through contemplation alone: Proverbs emphasises a busy, proactive and practical pursuit of wisdom in all situations of life. And, lest we fear that all this is beyond us, we may embrace the encouragement that if any of us 'lacks wisdom', we may 'ask God, who gives generously to all without finding fault, and it will be given' to us (James 1:5).

- Where do you see God's wisdom evident in creation? Can you apply such wisdom to your own creative activities?
- How do you deal with the apparent 'contradictions' in the book of Proverbs? Can you think of times in your own experience when similar situations have required quite different responses?
- How has your understanding of biblical wisdom been expanded over the last fortnight? Pray through the insights or questions that have arisen for you.

FURTHER READING

Craig G. Bartholomew and Ryan P. O'Dowd, *Old Testament Wisdom Literature: A Theological Introduction*, Apollos, 2011.

Daniel J. Estes, *Handbook on the Wisdom Books and Psalms*, Baker Academic, 2005.

Tremper Longman III and Peter Enns (eds.), *Dictionary of the Old Testament Wisdom, Poetry and Writings*, IVP, 2008.

Ernest Lucas, *Exploring the Old Testament Volume 3: The Psalms and Wisdom Literature*, SPCK, 2003.

Psalms 114 (113)—125 (124)

The beauty and the joy of reflecting on the Psalms stem from their variety. This prayer-book of Israel evolved over several centuries, reflecting the life and moods of Israel over those ages. Like any nation, Israel bore the scars of historical wounds and failures, as well as the treasured bloom of success and progress. All these have entered into the soul of Christianity and contributed to the way we see God and see ourselves in the sight of God.

This particular group of a dozen psalms is more varied than most, beginning with a highly imaginative reflection on the central event in Israel's history, then including a prayer made especially precious to Christians by the part it played in the life of Jesus, as well as the shortest of all the Psalms and the longest—a fervent meditation on the way to God marked out by the Law. After these, we enter upon the Songs of Ascent, a more homogeneous group of short, light-hearted pilgrimage songs, sung by Jews on the way to Jerusalem, and still by Christians on the way to the heavenly Jerusalem.

These notes are based on the Revised Grail Psalter and, unless otherwise stated, on the New Jerusalem Bible.

A note on numbering: The Revised Grail Psalter, in accordance with the Roman Catholic tradition, uses the numbering of the Greek version of the Psalms, rather than the Hebrew. In the Greek text, the Hebrew Psalms 9 and 10 are shown as a single psalm—Psalm 9. Thus the Greek version stays one number behind until Psalm 148. Because many Protestant versions adopt the Hebrew numbering (following Luther's preference), however, both numbers have been given in psalm references between 10 and 147. You will find the Hebrew number given first, with the Greek in brackets afterwards.

17–23 June

1 When Israel came forth from Egypt

Psalm 114 (113)

This psalm is an excited, playful and dramatic presentation of the basic story of the creation of Israel as God's people. We do not know exactly what happened at the exodus, for the story was told and retold in the Bible with the continual poetic exaggeration of folk-history, reaching its highest point in this playful psalm. The nearest approach to sober history may be Miriam's ancient triumph-song in Exodus 15: 'Horse and rider he has thrown into the sea...'. There must have been some dramatic escape from pursuing Egyptian forces, in which Moses and his straggle of runaway slaves were allowed to get across one of the lakes near what is now the Suez Canal, after which the pursuing forces were blocked. The 'walls of water' of later poetry need no more be taken literally than the Jordan actually turning back on its course (vv. 3, 5). The important factor was that the Lord rescued Israel from overwhelmingly powerful forces. Whatever the basic event, it was seen as the intervention of the strong right arm of the Lord, the introduction to his claiming the people as his own possession.

The continuance of this claim was always described in terms of thunder, lightning and earthquake on Sinai—the mysterious encounter of the covenant, by which God took Israel as his very own, establishing the law of life by which God's people should live. This is expressed in the second verse of today's psalm in a way that no decent translation could express. Judah became 'his holy thing', Israel 'his own possession', as though God hugged them to himself as if they were a precious treasure in which no other might share. Henceforth Israel was not like other nations but was dedicated to YHWH, sharing in YHWH's own awesome holiness.

There is a continual pairing of similar images throughout the psalm: Egypt/foreign people, Judah/Israel, sea/Jordan, mountains/hills, rock/flint and pool/spring. What brings delight to the psalm is the playful dramatic personification of the elements: the watery elements of sea and Jordan think better of their natural courses and cannily flee in terror; the solid elements of mountains and hills dance a jig like skittish lambs. These pictures come more easily in a culture where ideas of river-spirits and mountain-gods were familiar.

The numbering of the Psalms goes into freefall here, for the Greek version (the version of the Bible which, for the first 400 years of the Christian Church, was considered the only authentic text) joins into one psalm the Hebrew 114 and 115, despite the obvious differences between them. The reverse process occurs in Hebrew 116, which the Greek divides into two, meaning that the Greek ends up still one behind.

2 Not to us, O Lord, but to your name

Psalm 115 (113B)

The clue to this whole psalm lies in the first four verses, a contrast between the God of Israel and the man-made idols of the nations. These idols are very prominent in the thought of the psalmist, in a way reminiscent of the second part of Isaiah. This part of Isaiah (ch. 40—56) was written in Babylon during the exile, when Israel was brought face to face with a flourishing cult of idols.

Till then, the Israel had been content to proclaim YHWH as its God without concerning itself with other nations and their own protector-gods. It was generally assumed in the Near East that gods were territorial. So Naaman, the Syrian general cured of leprosy by Elisha, assumed that YHWH could be worshipped only on the soil of Israel, and accordingly took home to Damascus two donkey-loads of the soil to stand on while he prayed (2 Kings 5:17). (In the same way, that good Yorkshire-woman, St Helena, mother of the Emperor Constantine, took shiploads of soil from Jerusalem on which to build her Roman church, Santa Croce in Gerusalemme.) However, for Israel, the Babylonian exile was a great turning-point and deepening-point in their understanding of God. Confronted with the multiple and varied idols of Babylon, the author of Isaiah 40—56 pours out several satirical set-pieces, mocking the folly of worshipping carved idols. Such weird attempts to depict gods must have seemed even weirder to a people for whom all graven images were banned as a blasphemous limitation of the God who was totally other. Our Western culture and religion are so inured to classical, Renaissance and even Christian statuary that we can have little notion of the shock and horror that would have been occasioned by such attempts to pull the deity down to a humanly intelligible level. God is not meant to be understood, only worshipped. God is not meant to be comfortable, only awesome.

The exiles could only pray that some semblance of due glory might be given to the name, to the power enshrined in the unpronounceable name, for 'our God, the maker of heaven and earth, does whatever he wills' (v. 3). 'To your name give the glory' means the same as the first two petitions of the prayer Jesus taught his disciples: 'May your name be held holy, may your kingship come' (Luke 11:2). God's kingship can be fully recognised only when the gentle and loving power of his name is acknowledged by all the living and the dead. It was this that Jesus came to foster and demonstrate by his miracles and his teaching, and, finally, by the loving obedience of his death.

3 I love the Lord, for he has heard my cry

Psalm 116 (114—115)

Death, or rather deliverance from death, is written all over this psalm. The psalmist praises God for rescuing him from the snares of death, the anguish of Sheol (v. 3), in a way that seems to be more than just poetic imagery. The whole poem is a song of praise for rescue, expressed most strongly by raising the cup of salvation and making a thanksgiving sacrifice. Yet, in verse 15, in the second half of the psalm (unless the Greek translation was correct in splitting the psalm in two), he acknowledges that in the eyes of the Lord, the death of his faithful is precious. Does this mean that the Lord welcomes the death of his faithful? Or that the death of his faithful costs the Lord dear? Or, thirdly, that such a death is of major significance to the Lord? It is difficult to know, and none of these interpretations is wholly satisfactory.

Two other factors must bear on the interpretation of the psalm and its view of death. Firstly, belief in any sort of life with the Lord after death became explicit in Israel only in the second century before Christ, at the time of the Maccabean persecution. Nevertheless, there had existed long before then, at least since the time of the book of Job, a firm belief that the Lord's love for his chosen ones would never lapse or desert them: 'I know that my Redeemer lives… then in my flesh I shall see God' (Job 19:25–26, NRSV). The implications of this belief had not yet become explicit, although Psalm 73 can say, 'You were holding me by my right hand… and then you will lead me to glory' (vv. 23–24).

A second factor which may be borne in mind is that in 2 Corinthians 4:13–14 Paul quotes verse 10 (according to the Greek division, the first verse of Psalm 115) as the grounds of his hope and perseverance in the persecutions and worries of the apostolate: 'we, too, believe and therefore we, too, speak, realising that he who raised up the Lord Jesus will raise us up with Jesus in our turn'. Whatever its meaning in our own analysis, for Paul this psalm was an assurance of his hope in resurrection and life with Christ. We can afford to make this hope our own.

4 O praise the Lord, all you nations

Psalm 117 (116)

Is this little psalm worth commenting on, or can it simply be brushed under the carpet? Definitely worth commenting on! It gives the lie to any conception of a self-satisfied Israel, which thought of itself as the chosen people to the exclusion of all others. It also creates a puzzle for Christians.

From the first call of Abraham, as we have it now in Genesis 12:1–3, the choice of Abraham as a great nation implicated all peoples, who would 'bless themselves by him'. The choice cannot be seen as exclusive. Of course, the implications of this phrase took time to be fully understood, and it was not until the period of the Babylonian exile and beyond that Israel became sufficiently conscious of other nations to concern itself about their salvation. From then onwards, and already in the later chapters of Isaiah and the later prophets, it becomes a standard feature that all nations will come to draw salvation from Jerusalem: 'all the nations will stream to' the temple in Jerusalem (Isaiah 2:2). Jesus, having no form of transport other than his own two feet, had little contact with Gentiles, but challenged and then responded to the faith of the Syro-Phoenician who sought healing for her daughter, and crossed into the Gentile Decapolis to heal the Gerasene demoniac. This proved sufficient warrant for Peter and then Paul to extend the mission of the church into the Gentile world.

But how are all nations brought to praise the Lord? How can we say that all those who are saved are saved by Christ? Even if they have never even heard of Christ? Is 'No salvation outside the Church' a medieval European doctrine, exploded by the discovery of a world beyond Europe? Vatican II envisaged a series of concentric circles. The inner circle is those Christians in union with the Bishop of Rome; then there are wider bands of others who see their salvation in Christ, still others who acknowledge God under names such as YHWH or Allah, and finally believers who seek God under other signs and symbols. What of the other great world religions? The globalisation of the 21st century has brought us to realise the value of the great religions of the East and their positive function in promoting the commitment and qualities treasured by Christians. Can we say of such believers that, even though they have no historical link with Jesus Christ, nevertheless he is the mediator of their salvation? Are they, too, 'latent' or 'anonymous' Christians?

5 Go forward in procession with branches

Psalm 118 (117)

This festive psalm of celebration is clearly a processional chant. It begins and ends with a bracket of praise to the Lord 'for he is good' (vv. 1, 29) and centres on 'The Lord is my strength' (v. 14). The first half has many features of a triumph-song—for example, the introductory refrain, 'his mercy endures for ever', four times repeated; the appeal for help and the exaggerated claims of bloody victory (vv. 10–12), which are so typical of Near Eastern victory inscriptions of the time. The second half of the psalm develops the processional idea, as the cortège enters the temple.

Later rabbinic sources speak of this psalm as being used for the festival of Sukkoth or Tabernacles, which fits well with the mention of a procession with branches (v. 27), for this was, and is, the festival when Jews build and live in temporary shelters made of branches. These shelters commemorate the temporary homes of the Israelites during their 40 years of travelling through the desert of Sinai—a reminder that there is no abiding city on this earth.

In the New Testament context, this psalm brings us to Palm Sunday, both because of the branches and because of verse 26, 'Blest is he who comes in the name of the Lord', which was sung at Jesus' messianic entry into Jerusalem (Mark 11:9). Mark never worries about sequential chronology, and it is tempting to suggest that he took this scene from the approach to Sukkoth (which occurs in the autumn) and used it to illustrate Jesus' climactic entry on his final visit to Jerusalem. How aware were they, at the time, of the significance of this scene? Were Jesus and his disciples simply caught up in the celebrations of the festival, entering with the crowds of other pilgrims, but in such a way that the event later took on a messianic significance? Perhaps only later did they realise that the branches and the chant were directed to Jesus, as bringing the kingship of God to a new realism. John grants that the significance of Jesus' replacement of the temple building with the temple of his body (John 2:21) was appreciated only after the Spirit had been given. The Gospel accounts frequently show us the events of Jesus' life in the glow of inspired later understanding, imparted after Pentecost by reflection in the Spirit. Further reminiscence occurs in Jesus' reference to himself as the stone rejected by the builders, which has become the cornerstone (Psalm 118:22; see Mark 12:10).

6 Blessed are those whose way is blameless

Psalm 119 (118)

Who would sing a love-song about law? Yet this is just what the present psalm is! In Israel, the Law is a precious gift, a love-present from the Lord. In our modern conception of law, the law is considered as restrictive, compelling, something to be pushed to the limit, but for the Israelite it is liberating and a delight. The Law is the ideal present from the Lord. Obedience to the Law is not a tiresome obligation but a loving response to a loving gift, enabling the Israelite to approach God in loving humility and gratitude.

An ideal present continues to remind us of the giver, for it is chosen with attention, care and personal consideration, as a real mark of love between friends. Just so, the Law is God's charter of friendship, showing the Israelites what they must do and be if they are to be God's people. Thereby it shows the nature of God, for my presents show my own nature, what I value in my friend, and our most intimate means of communication with each other. Quite apart from the general nature of gift-giving, this becomes especially clear in the case of the Law, for so many of the precepts of the Law are framed by the imitation of God: 'Be holy as I am holy'; 'Remember the widow, the orphan and the immigrant among you, as I remembered you when you were widows, orphans and immigrants in Egypt.' Humankind is made in the image of God, male and female, but needs God's guidance to fulfil that image, and this is what the Law provides.

Notionally the Law was given by or, at least, through Moses (the paradigm case being the Ten Commandments written 'by the finger of God') but in fact it was the product of a series of decisions in particular instances of case law over several centuries. Many of the decisions were in conformity with the case law of surrounding peoples, but, in the case of the people of God, we would regard their adoption as being guided by the Holy Spirit. Two of the profound motivations behind them are the safeguarding of the holiness of God and the safeguarding of respect for every individual.

Such is the meaning of the affectionate and often even rapturous terms used of the Law in this long poem. As a poem, too, it is a tour de force. It falls into sections of eight verses, every verse in each section beginning with the same letter of the alphabet, and working successively through the alphabet. We have met this form of acrostic before—for example, in Psalms 25 (24) and 34 (33)—but in these cases only for single verses, not groups of eight verses. The terms used for the provisions of the Law are also remarkably varied, though it is difficult to weigh the precise differences between them.

Guidelines

A feature of many of this week's Psalms has been holiness—the awareness that Israel, with its commemorative festivals and the gift of the Law—was set apart as the special treasured possession of the awesome God, YHWH. Yet along with this awareness came a dawning realisation that Israel was intended to be the conduit of YHWH's blessing to all nations on earth.

The privilege of being dedicated to the Lord as his special possession belongs to Christians, too, through the mercy of Jesus Christ—'You are a chosen race, a royal priesthood, a holy nation, God's own people' (1 Peter 2:9)—as does the responsibility of extending that blessing to others. Jesus' great commission to the church is still to 'go… and make disciples of all nations, baptising them in the name of the Father and of the Son and of the Holy Spirit, and teaching them to obey everything that I have commanded you' (Matthew 28:19–20).

1 Friction in the tents of Qedar

Psalm 120 (119)

Here begin the 15 Psalms of Ascents, each of which has a heading: 'Song of Goings Up'. What precisely this means is unknown. A fairly late Jewish tradition associates these psalms with 15 steps leading up to the inner sanctuary of the temple; this may or may not be pure invention. They all make clear, however, that there was something special about going up to Jerusalem. One may well imagine that they were songs of joy sung by groups of pilgrims on their way up to Jerusalem for the great feasts, meeting up with other groups of pilgrims in greater and greater throngs, all coming from the strains and difficulties of living out their faith in unbelieving Gentile lands. Still today there are educated Jews who think that Jerusalem is the centre of the world in a quasi-territorial way (whereas everyone really knows that it is Little Muggleswick). The spirit of all these psalms is the enduring help of the Lord, beamed from Jerusalem and becoming ever more reassuring and comforting as its source is approached.

A clear feature of this psalm is the two place names in verse 5. They already betoken a meeting of pilgrims from faraway places, for Qedar seems to be located in northern Arabia, a symbol of distant desolation (Isaiah 42:11; Jeremiah 49:28–29), and Meshech considerably further north, in the area of the Caucasus. The two of them may be considered to stand for outlandish distant places. The other feature that the psalmist is glad to escape is labelled as deception and lying (v. 2). Were the two places inhabited only by compulsive liars? Rather than referring to persistent attempts to deceive the psalmist personally, he is more likely to be characterising idolatrous worship as deceit. This is seen in the prophets as a deliberate refusal to acknowledge the truth that YHWH is Lord of the world and all things (see, for example, Hosea 12:1; Jeremiah 9:4). In this case, the believer rejoices to get away from a twisted, distorted and so deceptive worldview. Disagreement over the ultimate truths of God and religion would also provide a better background for the friction described in the last verse of the psalm, the psalmist's longing for peace and the constant rebuttal with hostility.

2 I lift up my eyes to the mountains

Psalm 121 (120)

Holy mountains play a part in many religious rituals, fuelled by the inaccessibility, solitude, danger and inherent nobility of mountains. It is not just that the mountains are thought to be nearer heaven (as in the attempt to reach heaven with the tower of Babel), but that they remain mysterious and remote, unshakeable as the swirl of storm and thunder sweeps over them. Mount Olympus was the home of the gods in Greece, and the snow on Mount Kilimanjaro was held to be the sitting-cushion of the gods. The Hebrew–Christian tradition is no exception: the psalmist lifts up his eyes to the mountains, from where shall come his hope. (Grammatically, the second line could be understood as a question, but this would leave the first line oddly inconsequential.)

In Hebrew thought, the holy mountain *par excellence* is Mount Sinai. Tradition places this at Gebel Musa ('the mountain of Moses'), which is indeed an awesome mountain. In the burning heat of the Sinai desert, there is no earth to mitigate the severity, only rock and the sand produced by the silent friction of the winds. By midday even the camels are panting. The drama of the place is increased by the sombre shades of rock, some grey granite, others a rusty iron-ore hue, others again almost a sulphurous green, but all noble, as they soar in shards towards the sky. This is the traditional place where Israel underwent its formative experience of YHWH as its protector-God. Here also (but under the alternative name of Mount Horeb) the prophet Elijah met God in the 'voice of silence' and veiled his head in reverence (1 Kings 19:12–13).

In the New Testament, Moses and Elijah join Jesus on the holy mountain of the transfiguration, where the chosen three disciples experience his divinity before the passion. As the new Moses, the Matthaean Jesus gives his new Law on the holy mountain in the form of the Sermon on the Mount (ch. 5—7), just as Moses had given the Law on Sinai. Finally, as the awesome Danielic Son of Man, who has received 'all power in heaven and on earth' from the Ancient One (Daniel 7:13; Matthew 28:16–20), the risen Christ sends out his disciples from the holy mountain to teach all nations.

In Psalm 121, God is unsleeping (v. 4)—like the mountain, which is there as a guard, ever alert and unchanging. It provides shade from the sun in the day and, eerily, from the moon in the night. Majestic and unconquered, it guards our going and coming. The mountain is indeed a symbol of the protective power of God.

3 Pray for the peace of Jerusalem

Psalm 122 (121)

In two short verses, the psalmist envisages both the beginning of the pilgrimage, when he was invited to join the journey, and its end, standing within the gates of Jerusalem. This evokes diverse kinds of memories for me: the joy and excitement in an El Al plane when the signs for landing are switched on and the Hebrew song spreads swiftly through the passenger area: 'How good and pleasant it is, brothers seated together' (Psalm 133:1). Or a memory from the time when Jerusalem was still an international city—the sight of bent old men, lifetime pilgrims to Mecca, making the long and arduous journey in cattle-trucks, staggering their way into the second-holiest shrine of Islam, the Dome of the Rock. Or the view from Castel, the fortified hilltop, a day's march to the west of Jerusalem, from where the Crusaders, coming up from the coast, first caught sight of their goal on the skyline. 'It is there that the tribes go up, the tribes of the Lord.'

The etymology here given to the name is 'City of Peace', based on the word for 'peace', *shalom*, but a strong contender is 'City (or Foundation) of Salem', a Semitic god. Verse 6 gives a lovely medley of sounds based on *shalom*: *sha'alu shalom yerushalayim yishlehu ohavayik*, literally 'Ask peace for Jerusalem; they shall be at ease, those who love her.' The prayer for peace is appropriate, for Jerusalem is a city of strife and tension. Well known is the long-standing strife between Jews and Muslims (or is it between Israelis and Palestinians?) regularly fuelled by reprisals of various kinds by either side and total unwillingness to compromise. Only slightly less public is the constant hassle between different branches of Christianity, where the Holy Sepulchre itself is riven by strife between the three owners (Latin, Greek and Armenian) to the extent that the 'armistice' imposed by the Ottoman Empire two centuries ago still prescribes the allotment of times and places, and is administered by Muslims. Every hierarchical tradition of Christianity seems to have its own Patriarch—Catholic, Orthodox, Syrian, Latin, Greek, Armenian, Coptic, Ethiopic. Only Lutherans and Anglicans stand slightly aside, with a bishop 'in' Jerusalem rather than 'of' Jerusalem. Prayer for peace is sorely needed, for nowhere in the world is the scandal of Christian disunity, the failure of Christians to achieve the unity for which Christ prayed at the last supper, so obvious and so painful.

4 To you have I lifted up my eyes

Psalm 123 (122)

The chief metaphor in this psalm is striking—the close attention of the oriental servant or slave to the whim of his or her master, utterly attentive to the least indication of eyebrow or gesture. To recognise a slight movement may be a matter of life or death. Such, maintains the psalmist, is his attention to the will of the Lord. The first feature, then, is the utter dependence of humanity on God. We have no grounds for any comeback or protest to God: we can only accept what we are given.

The other striking feature is that this metaphor is expressed in female as well as male terms: the eyes of a slave-girl are fixed on the gestures of her mistress, just as the eyes of the male slave are on the gestures of his master. As we will soon see (with regard to Psalm 131), there is no sexual discrimination in God: men and women are treated alike, and God has neither male nor female characteristics to the exclusion of female or male features. God may, or must, be conceived in female terms no less than male, with feminine sensitivity as well as masculine strength, with female acceptance no less than masculine positive thrust.

In this poem, the longing for Zion comes into view in the longing to be free of the scorn and contempt of the arrogant. This may well be focusing on the contempt and unpopularity experienced by Jews in the diaspora among the Gentiles for their fidelity to the Lord. Both Gentile and Jewish sources attest the mockery undergone by Jews for their fidelity to their faith in the ancient as in the modern world. Faith always runs the risk of being mocked as credulity and gullibility. Religious practices always run the risk of appearing—and, indeed, of being—hypocritical. It has always been part of the vocation of the people of God, as the servant of the Lord, bearing witness to divine values, to be liable to mockery by those who do not share those values.

In the Greek version of the psalm, the poet twice in verse 3 uses the same words as would later be used by the Canaanite woman who sought healing for her daughter from Jesus, and would also become standard in the liturgy: *Kyrie eleison*, 'Lord, have mercy'. Just so, we put ourselves unreservedly in the hands of God.

5 The snare of the fowler

Psalm 124 (123)

Two striking images of threat dominate this psalm—the rushing water and the snare of the fowler. The Israelites were always afraid of the sea, not only because of its uncontrollable force but also because of their powerful creation story, in which God divided the waters to insert the world. The waters still surround the world, and God is still holding back the waters from engulfing it. If he ceased to do so, the mighty flood would implode the world. More practically frightening is the flood of water in a dry wadi. Within hours of the winter rains, the tidal wave of a flashflood, several metres high, can suddenly sweep down the dry bed of an enclosed canyon in the desert with inescapable force and the fury of 'raging waters'. The noted French biblical scholar Jean Steinmann was drowned with a score of other visitors to Petra by just such a flood in 1963.

I once saw a fowler's snare in operation on a patch of waste ground in Jerusalem. The fowler lays out on the ground a net some metres square, with hinged wings of similar netting. When the small birds are fluttering and squabbling over the bait placed in the middle of the net, the wings of netting are silently raised by means of strings and fall on the birds, trapping them inescapably. The psalmist prays to be delivered from just such a trap.

The dangers of a journey to Jerusalem would have been considerable. We may compare Paul's summary of risks confronting a traveller: 'I have been in danger from rivers, in danger from brigands, in danger from my own people and in danger from the Gentiles, in danger in the towns and in danger in the open country, in danger at sea and in danger from people masquerading as brothers' (2 Corinthians 11:26). On the roads and in the open countryside there was little rule of law, and kidnapping for the lucrative business of slavery was particularly rife during the final centuries before Christ. Those who could afford it would travel with an armed guard; those who could not might well be left without the succour of any good Samaritan 'when people rose against' them. They would be conscious of the need for divine protection especially at the beginning of the pilgrimage, decreasing as the throngs of pilgrims thickened and they could relax with thankfulness.

6 Those who put their trust in the Lord

Psalm 125 (124)

The original Jebusite city of Jerusalem, which David captured and made his capital, is indeed low-lying and nestles within a protective circle of hills. It is a low point on the spine of the country that runs north–south, and a crossing-point on the east–west road that runs from the coast. Before Solomon joined it to the hill to its north by his massive infill, the city was sufficiently isolated to form a defensive citadel but could never realistically claim to be higher than the other mountains. By a stroke of genius, David captured this strong but small city, lying between the northern territories (Saul's kingdom) and his own southern sphere of influence (Judah), and made it his capital, uniting the two territories around his own personal fiefdom. By an even greater stroke of genius, he installed the ark of the covenant there and, by so doing, made it also the Lord's capital, although he himself did not succeed in building the temple which was to make it the holy city of all holy cities. There was a certain air of patronage in his offer to build the Lord a house—an offer that the Lord refused, replying with the even more significant promise to build David a house (in the sense of dynasty) that would endure for ever.

As a holy city, Jerusalem's name is Zion. The Lord is enthroned in Zion, as several of the psalms relate. It is from Zion that the Lord will rule over all peoples. 'Zion' is Isaiah's preferred name for Jerusalem as the throne of the 'Holy One of Israel', which is Isaiah's favourite title for God. In the New Testament also, it is to Zion that the Messiah comes, riding on a donkey (Matthew 21:5, quoting Zechariah 9:9), and Mount Zion is the heavenly Jerusalem 'where the millions of angels have gathered for the festival' (Hebrews 12:22) and where the Lamb will take his stand with all those who are saved (Revelation 14:1).

At the end of time, Zion will be raised up by divine favour to dominate the surrounding hills, as a sign of divine exaltation rather than natural contours, a matter of eschatology rather than geography. Meanwhile, the circle of hills protecting Zion is a firm image of the Lord's sure protection for his holy and faithful people, those who put their trust in the Lord.

Guidelines

We have now reflected on nearly half the Psalms of Ascents, with their passionate yearning for Jerusalem, the holy city. In the Old Testament, this yearning focuses the longing for the kingship of God and the completion of the promises in the peace of the kingdom. For Christians, largely through the theology of pilgrimage in the letter to the Hebrews, such yearning is modified by the knowledge that the pilgrimage of the exodus to the promised land was incomplete. As Christians, we are still on pilgrimage towards the place of rest (Hebrews 4:1). In another sense, however, the goal has already been reached by the exaltation of Christ, so that in the Church everyone is a 'firstborn son' and a 'citizen of heaven' (Hebrews 12:23). This corresponds with the two Johannine eschatological viewpoints: in the Gospel of John the Church has replaced the temple as the dwelling-place of the Spirit (2:21), while, in the book of Revelation, the victory marked by the descent of the new Jerusalem (ch. 21) still lies in the future.

Luke 18—21

The next three weeks' readings continue the journey with Jesus towards Jerusalem, which began in 9:51. They are full of contrasts, including some of Luke's most memorable and appealing stories (for example, the Pharisee and the tax collector) and some of his most difficult and challenging words. Making this journey is rather like living through Psalm 23. Sometimes we are 'beside still waters' and at other times 'walking through the valley of the shadow of death' as the sense of oppression and death mounts (see 18:31–34; 19:40–44, 47–48; 20:13–19). In these chapters we see Jesus at his most winsome—for instance, when he responds to the parents rejected by the disciples as they seek to bring their children to him or when he engages so sympathetically and effectively with Zacchaeus, a chief tax collector. We also see him at his most challenging as he seeks to release the wealthy 'ruler' from the imprisonment of his wealth or as he faces the various opponents who come with their 'test-cases', hoping either to reveal his incompetence or to glean evidence that will help them do away with him.

Occasionally we might be glimpsing the anguish, even uncertainties, of Jesus himself. Perhaps, as he weeps over Jerusalem, we are allowed to see the deep spiritual pain that he carried as he foresaw the coming judgment on the holy city (19:41–42). Maybe, in 18:8, we catch his concern about whether the disciples will make it through all the testings to come, including his own brutal death and then the birth pangs of the new age, particularly as they seem so blind when he attempts to prepare them (18:34).

So, be ready to be drawn closer to Jesus, into a deeper and richer discipleship. Equally, however, be prepared for some intellectual and spiritual challenges. The road to Jerusalem is not an easy one.

1 The courage to pray

Luke 18:1–8

In many parts of the world, being a Christian is a very dangerous commitment. Persecution comes in many forms, from social disadvantage through to torture and death. It may involve a few vigilantes or it may reflect the policy and resources of the government or other powerful agents. In some situations, it comes as family pressure, with all the additional pain that stems from a sense of misunderstanding, shame and isolation; in others it can be intensified by the impersonal nature of the oppressors. Wherever and however it takes place, the Christian will live with a gnawing sense of vulnerability.

That sense of vulnerability was typical for a widow in Jesus' day. If she had no one to support and defend her, she was powerless. If someone decided to remove her property and possessions, or even molest her, she was truly exposed and helpless. Indeed, her status as a widow might be used to discredit her: surely God was punishing her for misdemeanours!

This was the challenge facing the widow in Jesus' parable. In addition to being portrayed as a rather humorous character, she is shown to be extremely brave and determined, constantly 'door-stepping' this powerful figure in her local community—the judge. And this is, I think, the central issue. She has no alternative; furthermore, even though it isn't demonstrated in practice by the judge who has 'no fear of God and no respect for anyone' (v. 4), she is convinced that justice is built into the universe.

For the widow, her plea is a life-or-death issue, so she invests her whole self in tackling the judge. So, when the disciples feel the same intense level of vulnerability as they face both Roman and Jewish persecution, or when pressure is applied from their families or social networks, then their response is to be parallel. They must constantly beseech God for help. If the widow had focused on her feelings of powerlessness, she would not have bothered. If she had depended on human logic about the probability of receiving a response from this harsh judge to her petty problems, when she couldn't afford to bribe him, she would not have persisted.

So Christians, whether under persecution or simply facing problems they can't resolve, need to apply themselves to prayer, no matter what their feelings or the logic of the situation.

2 The humility to pray

Luke 18:9–14

In 2012 we celebrated the 200th anniversary of the birth of Charles Dickens, noted for his ability to stimulate social change through his novels. At the heart of his stories are a perceptive observation of human characters and behaviour and the ability to encapsulate them in word-pictures. Jesus was even more brilliant at this! There are few better examples than his depiction of the Pharisee in the temple.

It is perhaps alarming to think that the Pharisee might score highly on some contemporary approaches to prayer, not least because there is no intercessory element to his prayer. He requests nothing either for himself or others. He has no need for a *deus ex machina* who will intervene in human, social and cosmic affairs. His prayer is also positive: it is an expression of thanks. It is not full of soul-searching; nor does he manifest an obsession with guilt, confession and the desire for forgiveness. Rather, prayer is the Pharisee's aid to self-awareness; it is his way of recognising his own good qualities!

By contrast, the tax collector's few words indicate his naive and impoverished view of both God and himself: 'God, be merciful to me, a sinner.' His words are matched, even superseded, by his rituals. He distances himself and is cowed down by his view of God: he won't even lift his eyes towards God. He has a very demeaning self-understanding: he 'beats his breast', a well-known way in the East to indicate unworthiness and self-humiliation. From a contemporary point of view, he is a prime example of the harm that religion can do to people! (Indeed, unless such a deep sense of unworthiness is met by the forgiving grace of God, it may well cause damage.)

Jesus' assessment, however, may challenge these contemporary views of prayer, the person and God. For Jesus, our attitude before God is of primary importance, because it indicates whether we know God or not.

Once we understand God as Jesus did, as the perfect one whose will is to be obeyed and implemented on earth, the one to whom all glory should be ascribed, then the only proper human response is worship, submission and a deep humility because of our sinfulness as well as our finitude. When we admit our sinfulness, as the tax collector did, it opens God's heart to us, so that we are 'justified' in his view (v. 14).

3 A revealing incident

Luke 18:15–17

Jesus was on a mission to proclaim 'the year of the Lord's favour' and so to heal the sick and set captives free (Luke 4:18–21). The disciples had been sent out as part of the fulfilment of his mission (10:1–12), and Jesus was now on his way to Jerusalem to bring it to completion. The disciples knew how urgent this mission was, for Jesus had issued many challenges on that issue. It was all about the kingdom of God.

Not surprisingly, then, they thought they were doing the right thing when they 'sternly ordered' people not to hinder the onward progress of Jesus. These people were wanting Jesus to touch their children. They were not bringing him life-and-death cases that needed healing. They were merely demonstrating their superstitious attitudes, wanting the protective touch of a miracle-worker, as they no doubt perceived him. Allowing these people to intrude on Jesus' mission would not only hold him up; it would send out all the wrong messages to the crowds.

This incident reveals just how easy it is for those who are closest to Jesus to misunderstand him and act in ways that deny his mission. The kingdom of God was not only for the brave fishermen who had become disciples of the increasingly famous rabbi; it is not reserved for the spiritual élite or those with the energy and ability to assist Jesus in his mission.

'Let the little children come to me... for it is to such as these that the kingdom of God belongs' (v. 16). This incident reveals Jesus' understanding about those who are most welcome into the kingdom—although today's disciples are still puzzled by the question of which key quality in children opens up the kingdom of God to them. Is it their trustfulness, their vulnerability, their teachability, their expectancy, their receptivity, their innocence or their simplicity? Maybe we can't always be sure we know exactly what Jesus wants or what he thinks about contemporary challenges and issues.

4 A Jewish leader

Luke 18:18–30

How do you help people to open up to the reality of God, when they are secure, used to receiving approval and respect, and fixed in their own mindset? That was the challenge that faced Jesus when a Jewish leader approached him with a very proper question: 'Good teacher, what must I do to inherit eternal life?' (v. 18).

Was this an academic, theological question or was it an existential, spiritual question? It certainly appears to be more than just a trick question. The man is serious about his own life, its purpose and its future. His commitment to law observance (v. 21) indicates his sincerity. But is this enough?

According to Jesus, 'No'. One more thing is necessary. 'One more?' we might ask in the light of the passage. Surely there are at least two—selling all his possessions and benefiting the poor, and then following Jesus. However, Jesus clearly states, 'There is still one thing lacking' (v. 22). So what is it?

This encounter, in Luke's account, is very carefully structured (see Kenneth E. Bailey, *Through Peasant Eyes*, Chapter 10, for one analysis). It begins and ends with a reference to 'eternal life' (vv. 18, 30), while, in between, Jesus speaks of the 'kingdom of God' (vv. 24, 29). For this enquiring Jew, 'eternal life' did not mean 'everlasting bliss' or 'the state of immutability of the soul'. In Jewish thought, to have 'eternal life' was to live in the world of God's new creation, as opposed to the present world order. In that new world, evil would be banished, God's intentions for his creation would be established and secured, and God's will would be perfectly carried out. So 'eternal life' has the same meaning as, in Jesus' words, 'the kingdom of God'. But the second time Jesus uses the latter expression in this passage (v. 29), he is using it as the equivalent of Peter's words, 'we have... followed you'. Once again, Jesus is eliding commitment to himself with 'the kingdom of God'.

So this is the 'one thing' necessary—commitment to Jesus as the centre of God's kingdom. For the Jewish enquirer, disposing of his possessions is simply(!) the necessary precursor to that commitment. Rightly understood, this passage is not only a huge challenge to most of us in the affluent world, but also a claim by Jesus to the highest possible status.

5 Double blindness

Luke 18:31–43

Verses 31–34 form the sixth prediction of Jesus' coming death (see 9:22, 44; 12:50; 13:32–33; 17:25). It serves several functions here. Primarily it underlines the reason for the journey to Jerusalem, which began way back in chapter 9. Like a repeated musical theme, it restores the focus of the composition and provides a platform for new developments. It also underlines for us the amazing courage of Jesus. While rich lawyers are deciding that they can't part with their wealth, and forthright disciples are underlining the sacrifices they have made in leaving home, Jesus lives with the constant and growing awareness of the horror of his end and the total abandonment of life that he is making. This not only puts the purpose of this journey to Jerusalem into proper perspective; it puts the 'sacrifices' we make for Jesus there, too.

This version of Jesus' prediction clarifies many of the details. Its placement is also highly appropriate in this context. Jesus has just promised Peter and all the disciples that any sacrifice they might make will be fully rewarded in this age and the age to come. The reference to the resurrection (v. 33) indicates a recognition that his rising again will be the start of this 'new age': the disciples' rewards will be brought about by the cost of Jesus' gruesome death. But it also indicates Jesus' understanding that the same pattern applies to him, too. His act of total abandonment of his life, and his commitment to his Father, will bring in the kingdom, the heart of his existence.

Then, with three different phrases, Luke underlines the inability of the disciples to take in what Jesus has been saying (v. 34: 'understood nothing'; 'was hidden from them'; 'did not grasp'). It is worth noting how similar are the comments on those who make the journey from Jerusalem to Emmaus, in Luke 24:13–35. In stark contrast, however, is the blind beggar whom Jesus heals (vv. 35–43). He understands that Jesus is 'the Son of David' who can restore God's broken creation by giving him back his sight. He understands that Jesus can show him mercy, just as God could, so he will allow nothing to prevent him seizing the opportunity. His immediate response to his healing is to 'glorify God', which sets off a chain reaction of praise (v. 43). How true it is that 'the blind see'!

6 The God of the impossible

Luke 19:1–10

The disciples' desperate question to Jesus in 18:26, 'Then, who can be saved?' now receives a demonstrable answer. Jesus has claimed that 'what is impossible for mortals is possible for God' (18:27), and now he shows how it happens.

Imagine you are the intended reader of Luke's Gospel—'most excellent Theophilus'. You are wealthy, in a respected social position; you are perhaps a 'God-fearer' (a non-Jew but someone who is drawn to the Jewish God). Luke's account of Jesus contains some encouragements for you—for instance, his description of the centurion who loves the Jewish people, and to whom Jesus responds positively, healing the man's servant without being physically present (7:1–10). But there is much that is depressing, especially Jesus' negative response to those who are wealthy. You have just heard that it is impossible for the rich to enter the kingdom unless God intervenes (18:26–27).

Now you read about Zacchaeus. Like you, he is in a liminal position, with a foot in two worlds, so to speak: Jericho was a border town and tax collectors were considered unclean and rejected by their fellow Jews. Zacchaeus, however, is a 'chief tax collector', so he too has social status and is rich. What this story shows you is that Jesus responds to your desire to encounter him and that your wealth need not prohibit that encounter. God is at work in Jesus to 'save' this rich man, and it can happen 'today' (mentioned twice, in verses 5 and 9).

It also shows how you will know that Jesus has visited you. Zacchaeus welcomed Jesus 'happily', or with joy (v. 6). Joy is a frequent theme of this Gospel (see 1:14; 10:20; 13:17; 15:5, 32; 19:37; 24:41) and indicates the appropriate response to God's salvific intervention. In Acts, it is also a sign of the Spirit's presence. Zacchaeus' freedom to be generous with his acquired wealth is another indicator of salvation. He demonstrates his new freedom in two ways—by giving away half his riches to the poor (v. 8) and by making very generous recompense to those he has defrauded. The law required an additional 20 per cent (Leviticus 5:16) and the rabbis occasionally demanded 40 per cent. A 'fourfold' repayment was almost unprecedented (but see Exodus 22:1; 2 Samuel 12:6).

Finally, you are embraced by the words of Jesus: 'For the Son of Man came to seek out and to save the lost' (v. 10). While the words of 18:25 made you feel a hopeless case, these words rescue you. But you also see that Jesus is doing God's work, and you will soon learn the real cost of your rescue by Jesus.

Guidelines

I invite you to consider two things that can significantly damage people, which find focus in this week's readings.

The first is religion. The picture of the wretched 'sinner' in the temple grovelling before God, overwhelmed by his own plight, is one illustration. We all need to be aware that there are some sensitive people who can easily be suppressed or depressed by the things we do in churches. These can range from 'perfectionist' views of family through to the sense of condemnation that can arise from some styles of preaching. But the self-righteous Pharisee is, according to Jesus, even more badly damaged by his sense of high achievement through religion. He is also filled with an unwarranted self-confidence about the sort of behaviour that God approves; and the disciples would soon discover that they hadn't got everything sorted either (18:15–17). Are we ourselves prone to either response to a religious environment? What about other people in our home group or church? More importantly, what can we do to adjust our language (including the selection of hymns and songs), our actions and our attitudes to minimise these risks?

The second danger is wealth. Recently I heard a minister say that all of us, even the poorest in England, are among the top two per cent of the world's wealthy people. If so, we are all in danger of being trapped by our wealth, hindered from engaging fully with God because we do not recognise our essential dependence on him. Do we need to renew our encounter with Jesus, so that we can be freed to live and love as Zacchaeus was? Perhaps inviting the Holy Spirit to renew your longing for intimacy with Jesus is a good place to start.

In the end, and in several ways, it was religion and wealth that took Jesus to the cross. Yet neither need destroy us, for through the cross Christ sets us free.

1 Gaining and using 'royal power'

Luke 19:11–27

From a well-loved story of human redemption through encounter with Jesus, we turn to a rather complex and disturbing parable. 'As for these enemies of mine… bring them here and slaughter them in my presence' (v. 27). Is this the same Jesus who proclaimed salvation to Zacchaeus?

Luke helpfully provides two motivations for the telling of this story (v. 11). First, Jesus is near Jerusalem and, second, some of his listeners are anticipating the imminent arrival of the kingdom.

First we can remind ourselves that the reference to Jerusalem is not primarily geographic; it has to do with the means of salvation. Jerusalem is where God's redemptive purposes will be enacted through the death of Christ. But Christ's death means that he will be going away to receive royal authorisation, first through his reception by God after death (see 23:42–43) and then through his ascension (24:51–52; Acts 1:6–11). It is important to understand the dynamics in the parable: the nobleman does not go away to 'get royal power' over another country—say, by conquest or even patronage. He is going to the seat of power for the whole region (for example, to Caesar) to be designated as the one who has the right to rule back home (in, say, Judea). So his absence from his own lands is necessary to gain regal and legal rights to rule over the territory he has (temporarily) left behind. He will be coming back to exercise his new royal authority.

Hence the second reason for the story. There were probably those who, in the timeline of this account, anticipated the arrival of God's kingdom during that very Passover. There were also, probably, some who anticipated it in Luke's own timeline, perhaps in connection with the Roman threats around AD70. Neither group was correct; but the first disciples and the early Christians were not to think that either the death of Jesus or his later absence undermined the truth that one day he would return as king and exercise his kingdom rule. When that day came, it would be a time for proper restitution. Faithful and unfaithful Christian living would receive appropriate recognition and so would downright opposition to Jesus. This was for an unknown, but certain, future. It was not for Christians or Romans to carry out God's prerogative. Such judgment was only to be carried out in the restored kingdom and in the direct presence of Jesus.

2 Almost there

Luke 19:28–40

This is one of the most vivid and memorable scenes in all the Gospels. Its vibrancy, colour and joyful acknowledgment of Jesus lodge easily in our minds. The donkey and the waving palm branches, accompanied by a psalmic chorus, appeal to so many senses at once.

Most of us refer to this episode as 'the triumphal entry', meaning Jesus' entry into Jerusalem. That is certainly how Matthew presents it: 'When he entered Jerusalem' follows immediately after the last 'Hosanna' (21:9–10) and the impression is given that the excitement of the crowd continues within Jerusalem. Mark is almost as proximate: 'Then he entered Jerusalem' follows the last 'Hosanna' (11:10–11), but then comes a semi-hiatus with 'and went into the temple'. For Luke, however, there is much more of a gap after the accolades from the crowds. First there is an altercation with the Pharisees (v. 39–40) and then Jesus pauses to weep for the future fate of Jerusalem (vv. 41–44). By the time he enters the temple (v. 45), the noise of the jubilant crowd has become a rather distant memory.

Luke seems to make the progress to Jerusalem deliberate and in stages, from 18:31 to 19:45: '"We are going up to Jerusalem" … As he approached Jericho… He entered Jericho and was passing through it… Because he was near Jerusalem… He went on ahead, going up to Jerusalem… As he was now approaching the path down from the Mount of Olives… As he came near and saw the city, he wept over it… Then he entered the temple…' It reads like a pilgrim's travelogue.

All the usual elements of the story of Jesus' entry into Jerusalem are here in Luke, but the overall impact has changed. Only Luke has this verse: 'The whole multitude of the disciples began to praise God joyfully with a loud voice for all the deeds of power that they had seen' (v. 37). For him, the praise is much more clearly formed. It comes from disciples, not just a crowd. It is not simply the response of an excited pilgrim throng to the sight of Jesus; it is expressed because they have an informed recognition that Jesus is God's agent for amazing miracles. 'Deeds of power' might be predictive of military intervention, too, but Luke has indicated in many ways that this will not be the case. So here he underlines the fact that this crowd rejoices not because of future hopes of messianic intervention (as is perhaps the case in Matthew and Mark) but because of the healings and redemptive encounters he has already performed. 'They had seen' (v. 37) are critically significant words, and they become even more important in view of what happens next.

3 Missed opportunities

Luke 19:41–44

'He wept over it' (v. 41). Jesus must have been very puzzling at times to his followers. He has just pulled off a remarkable pageant and received jubilant recognition. Now, as he gets to see Jerusalem, he starts to weep.

For the pilgrims of Psalm 122, tears might have been understandable—tears of relief and joy at the end of an arduous and costly journey. The city that was the focus of all their hopes was now in view. Soon they would be in the temple with all their fellow worshippers, receiving the blessing and forgiveness of God. Jerusalem was the aim of their lives.

For Jesus, though, these are not tears of relief or joy. Rather, they are tears of prophetic lament. We might be tempted to see in them a natural human reaction—Jesus coming to terms with his own death, or grieving as he thinks about the fate that awaits Jerusalem, or expressing sorrow that the city and its harsh religious leaders have missed their last opportunity—but there is more.

We should see here that Jesus is acting out a prophetic sign. Jesus is often thought of as a prophet by his contemporaries, and with good reason (see, for example, 9:18–20). The prophets not only called people back to God's ways, gathered disciples, spoke in parables and predicted the future judgment of God; they also enacted that judgment in visible signs. Isaiah, Jeremiah and, most of all, Ezekiel did so—and that is what Jesus is doing.

This 'sign' perhaps serves a similar function to the story of the cursing of the fig tree, found in Matthew (21:18–19) and Mark (11:12–14, 20–21) but omitted by Luke. That story occurs in connection with Jesus' 'cleansing of the temple', and is probably another way of portraying the fate that awaited Jerusalem, the fig tree being a symbol for the Jewish temple worship—apparently flourishing but ultimately fruitless, and so subject to God's judgment.

Through his act of prophetic weeping, then, Jesus was emphasising the reality of the impending judgment of God. Jesus understood the fact that, in crucifying him, the leaders were rejecting God's last invitation to repent. Of course, prophetic words and signs also gave people a final opportunity to change their ways.

4 The Lord comes to the temple

Luke 19:45–48

Luke's account of the cleansing of the temple is much shorter than in any of the other Gospels (see Mark 11:15–19; Matthew 21:12–17 and especially John 2:13–22). Why might this be? Perhaps it was because Luke wanted to play down the disruptive and socially disturbing elements within the Jesus story. This would have special relevance if Theophilus was a peace-loving person (a supporter of the *Pax Romana*). Luke's somewhat minimalist account could then be understood, but his presentation would also indicate his wisdom and astuteness in fulfilling his Gospel intentions.

It may also have been because the temple was no longer a major issue for Luke's readers: from a historical perspective, perhaps the temple had already been destroyed by the Romans. Just previously in the chapter (19:43–44), Luke has recorded Jesus as predicting a total demolition of the temple. Compared with the brutality of this destruction, perhaps Jesus' actions were considered so mild as hardly to warrant any attention. Theologically, too, the temple rituals were no longer valid as a way of being reconciled with God; nor was any such 'commercial activity' hindering Gentiles from coming to faith through Jesus and joining his church. Jesus emphasises the temple as 'a house of prayer' here (v. 46) but, unlike Mark (11:17), Luke does not add '… for all the nations'. (Luke is in agreement with Matthew here, and John doesn't use the quotation at all.) The omission of 'for all the nations' would make sense both historically and theologically after AD70.

There are at least four ways in which Jesus' action can be viewed. From the perspective of the animal sellers and money changers, it must have seemed like the action of an angry young man. It also appeared like a social protest against the commercialism that had developed around the need for pure animals and money (see Deuteronomy 15:20–21; Malachi 1:6–8): the references to 'marketplace' (in John) and 'den of robbers', as here, support that idea. It should also be viewed as 'prophetic symbolism', especially in Luke's Gospel, coming immediately after Jesus' tears over Jerusalem. Finally, for Jesus and, probably, the disciples after the resurrection, it was a hidden messianic claim (see Malachi 3:1–4). This claim probably lies behind the story's treatment in John's Gospel.

5 By what authority?

Luke 20:1–8

The issue of authority was, and always will be, an important issue. In Luke 7:1–10, the centurion knew he was under authority (ultimately, that of Caesar) so he could command others—even to kill—and expect to be obeyed. He therefore recognised that Jesus was under God's authority and so could even command healing. Authority is rather like electricity: you don't have to be able to see it for it to be potent.

Jesus had challenged the 'authorities' by clearing out the people involved in the buying and selling of animals for sacrifice, but by what authority did he do this? Was it by Roman authority—was he secretly in league with the Procurator? If not, how did he have the right? He was telling the good news of the kingdom: who gave him the authority for that?

It is unlikely that his right to teach was being questioned here, because, as far as we know, there was not yet any formal process for training and becoming a rabbi. But Jesus was announcing that the kingdom of God was imminent. How did he know? Had God appointed him to be a prophet? (This was a common opinion: see 9:18–20; 22:63–65). If so, what evidence did he have for this? Part of the good news was his ability to heal (see 4:18), and his exorcisms were also an issue for debate. Did he derive his authority to do these things from Beelzebub (see Luke 11:14–23)? That was the smear campaign!

Those who ran Jerusalem on the Jewish side, and also oversaw the temple system, had to work very hard to keep the balance of authority right. If they upset Pilate or Herod by appearing to be at all rebellious, they would be in serious trouble. If they appeared to be too compliant, to the point of sacrificing their Jewish privileges (for instance, about allowing no Gentiles in the inner sections of the temple), the population could become restive, especially at Passover time, which celebrated Israel's deliverance from the oppression of Egypt.

The difficulty for Jesus was that if he claimed that his authority was from God, he could be accused of blasphemy (see 22:66–71). However, if he denied that God was the source of his authority, he could probably be arrested as an imposter. Hence the approach that Jesus took, throwing the challenge back to the chief priests, scribes and elders. In addition, Philippians 2:6–8 reminds us that Jesus would not grasp at, claim or project the truth that he was equal to God and that therefore his authority came from God. We are all called to weigh the evidence and decide for ourselves.

6 The vineyard of Israel

Luke 20:9–18

Within this parable of the vineyard and the tenant farmers lies a clue to Jesus' authority. It could only be a clue because politically and theologically overt claims to divine authority were dubious. However, he makes the point without explicitly identifying himself with the owner's 'beloved son'.

It is worth asking ourselves where the hearers' natural sympathies would lie, as this affects the impact of the parable. For many, perhaps the majority of us, our sympathy lies with the owner of the vineyard. After all, unlike the first hearers, we know how the story ends, with the ungrateful and murderous behaviour of the tenant farmers. We also know that the vineyard symbolises the nation of Israel (Isaiah 5:1–7) and that Israel is unresponsive and ungrateful to God. But for Jesus' first hearers, their sympathies would have been with the tenant farmers, as might be the case with people in the Amazon rainforest who have their land seized by a multinational logging company. So Jesus has to lure the hearts and minds of his hearers away from supporting the tenants (dominated by a distant wealthy landowner as they seek to eke out a meagre living from their land) to sympathising with the owner, whose 'beloved son' has been killed. This was the same journey on which he longed to take the people of Jerusalem, so that they could avoid the destruction that awaited them (19:41–44).

When the listeners exclaim, 'Heaven forbid!' in verse 16, the immediate cause of their horror is the threat that the tenants will be destroyed and the land taken away from them. Perhaps they are revealing where their natural sympathies lie, but more probably they recognise Jesus' suggestion that the Jews will lose their lands. Just maybe, their horror goes further back to verses 14–15, where the tenants plot and carry out their murder of the son. Within their culture, however, perhaps they could easily imagine such a thing happening, for 'When land belonged to someone without an heir, inheritance followed a certain custom: when the owner died, the land usually passed on to those who worked the land' (D.L. Bock, *Luke*, New Testament Commentary, IVP, 1994, p. 322.)

However we interpret the listeners' reaction, the message is clear that acting without taking God fully into account could only bring disaster (vv. 17–18).

Guidelines

One of the important topics that emerge from this week's readings is that of Christ's authority. He behaves in strange ways, weeping as he approaches Jerusalem, then clearing the temple courtyard of all the paraphernalia of sacrifice and institutional religion. He also makes striking and severe predictions through his parables. We ought to have sympathy for the position of the Jewish leaders: Jesus was very difficult to handle. He seemed to have authority given him by the people through their attention and adulation, making him a kind of celebrity. But (the leaders may have thought) it was easy for Jesus: he didn't have a complex temple system to run, or delicate issues of 'church and state' to negotiate on a daily basis.

The leaders also had their own authority, derived from their committed and disciplined religious lives and endorsed by years of practical success at minimising Roman interference. They needed to preserve their authority to benefit the nation and to honour God. This is how the situation must have seemed to them, even if they also wanted that authority for their own sakes.

This week's readings can prompt us to re-examine our own understanding of our authority as leaders, in the church and elsewhere. Where does it come from? Why do we need it or seek to preserve it? Do we understand it and use it in a fully Christ-like way? In the end, Jesus had authority only because he was carrying out God's purposes and was willing to pay the ultimate sacrifice to do so.

We may also wish to pray for our political and religious leaders, as well as those whose exercise of authority troubles us or those who constantly seem to challenge, resent or undermine our own.

1 Hypocrisy and taxes

Luke 20:19–26

Here we have another question about 'authority', but now it has become a life-and-death issue. The 'scribes and chief priests', who have been significantly affronted by the parable that Jesus has told against them, want to hand Jesus over to Pilate's authority. Hidden here is an issue that will emerge more clearly during the trial process for Jesus. These leading Jews had little independent authority. When it came to the death penalty, they needed the Roman governor's decision: they were under his authority.

So, they send out spies (v. 20). Other Gospels (see Matthew 22:16; Mark 12:13) say that they send disciples of the Pharisees and Herodians (the Pharisees represent those who recognise the supreme authority of God, while the Herodians are those who recognise, more pragmatically, the authority of Rome), but they are spies because they are tasked with reporting any incriminating evidence to their paymasters.

The question they are charged with putting to Jesus is also about authority. Paying taxes is a costly way of acknowledging authority. Every conquering country put burdens of taxation on people, but the Jews paid their taxes to God, via the temple, because they acknowledged God's authority over them (in theory!).

Politicians and corporations spend large sums of money on training their staff to handle aggressive media interviewers. Jesus knew how to do it, and somehow always managed to turn the tables on those trying to catch him out. Moreover, in the process he exposed their hypocrisy. The fact that his inquisitors carried money with the image of Caesar's head on it was proof that they were already accepting his authority—even though there had been serious objections when Pilate brought images of the emperor into Jerusalem by night (see *Lion Handbook to the Bible*, 1999 edition, p. 534).

What is the import of Jesus' response: 'Give to the emperor the things that are the emperor's, and to God the things that are God's' (v. 25)? Is this proof that politics and religion should never be mixed? Certainly not! To start with, the one issuing this edict (and so exercising the authority) is 'from God'. Thus, the ultimate authority is God's but he allows for the exercise of authority through intermediaries in the political and civic spheres.

2 False assumptions

Luke 20:27–40

Sometimes details really matter, and that is the case for a full understanding of this debate.

Luke not only tells us who brought the next challenging question to Jesus but also provides us with the necessary detail to facilitate a proper understanding. The questioners were Sadducees, who tended to be from the wealthy aristocracy. They taught that 'there is no resurrection' (v. 27). This is the crucial piece of information that Theophilus and many later readers were unlikely to know. There is a second detail that aids understanding, which is that the Sadducees would only accept the Torah, the five Books of Moses, as carrying divine authority.

In both these respects they differed from the Pharisees, although they did share an antipathy to Jesus and a willingness to debate about minutiae. Here, however, they make use of a more creative device: they tell a story. A woman's husband dies leaving her childless, and so, according to the law of Levirate marriage, her husband's brother marries her (see Deuteronomy 25:5 and Ruth 4 for a flavour of the inheritance issues underlying this law). This happens six more times, so the woman has had seven husbands. Who will have conjugal rights in heaven? Will there be a major family feud? The Sadducees are employing a *reductio ad absurdum* argument. Clearly the end game is ludicrous; hence the premise that there is life after resurrection must be false.

Unfortunately for them, Jesus easily exposes their false premise: in the age to come, people 'neither marry nor are given in marriage' (v. 35). The false assumption is that the resurrection life is simply an extension of this one, with all its family and social networks. This is an alert to all of us. As soon as we project our experiences here into God's new future, we may well be misleading ourselves. Many of the conundrums we think about, from 'Will there be animals?' to 'How will we talk to so many people at once?', may not apply. Life will be so different that a considerable degree of restraint and agnosticism is required by us all. What is important, Jesus tells us, is that we cannot die and we will be 'children of God' (v. 36)—not only precious to him but sharing his nature.

Jesus then establishes, from the Sadducees' own authoritative scriptures, that the resurrection is implied within the Torah. So Jesus not only unpicks their argument but also has the courtesy to point them to the truth through their own scriptures.

One more detail! Some of the scribes acknowledge that Jesus has responded well (v. 39). Almost certainly, these are not the Sadducees capitulating but their theological enemies, the Pharisees, enjoying their 'humiliation'.

3 Convictions

Luke 20:41–47

Now we have Jesus moving on to the attack. In two very different ways, he establishes victory in the legal contest between himself and his opponents.

First he presents the scribes with a question they can't answer. Although the audience is not specified and the question might have been put to the Sadducees as well, this seems unlikely, as the basis for Jesus' scriptural reasoning is a passage from Psalm 110, and not the Torah.

It is also unlikely that the point of contention is the Davidic descent of the Messiah. While we know from places like Qumran that there were other conceptions of the Messiah's origins, the Davidic descent seems to have been important for Luke and Jesus, as well as the Pharisees (see Luke 1:27, 69; 2:4, 11; 3:31; 18:38–39). So the critical issue is to show that the Messiah was much greater than David but, perhaps by implication, greater in a different way—not so much an empire builder by military means but a kingdom builder by God's means. Jesus' opponents have no answer to his question.

Psalm 110 was a significant psalm for the early church in its debates with Judaism, as its frequent quotation indicates, and here its use goes back to Jesus. The reference to a figure sitting 'at my right hand' was taken up in the early church's understanding of Jesus' ascension and exaltation, although the point about humiliating and destroying his enemies was not! Here it perhaps helps to prepare us for Jesus' prediction of the destruction of the temple and Jerusalem, in chapter 21. Importantly, though, this destructive work is seen as a task not for the Messiah but for his Lord—that is, God. Perhaps this, too, was significant in Luke's presentation of the innocence of Jesus. Not only could his critics not silence him; they had no answer to his questions.

Jesus' second victory is achieved by unmasking the hypocrisy of the scribes. In the briefest of pen portraits, he deftly presents the scandal. He draws three pictures, each with two elements. In the first, the ostentation of the scribes is presented as they parade outside (long garments flowing, in the marketplace); the second portrays a similar ostentation as they seek adulation inside (at banquets and in the synagogue). The final picture presents two contrasting elements: the scribes 'devour' widows' property and say long prayers. The only connection is the use of the mouth (taking the metaphor of 'devouring' seriously!). In this they reveal that, rather than being genuinely pious and honourable, they are actually vicious wild animals.

Jesus here does not condemn the scribes by pronouncing 'woes' on them as he did in Luke 11; rather, he presents them as a warning to his disciples.

4 Generous giving

Luke 21:1–11

TV and radio presenters often seek to link disparate parts of their programme together using a device known as a 'segue'—a connecting theme or phrase. Here, there seems to be little in common between people moving around the Court of the Women, placing their gifts in the large receptacles, and the violence of wars and earthquakes. But the segue is 'gifts', for it is the observation that the temple has been adorned with 'gifts dedicated to God' (v. 5) that prompts Jesus to move into his pronouncement of doom on the temple and then his portrayal of the destruction of Jerusalem.

Today we focus on the account of the poor widow. Both in his parables and in his pen portraits (for example, of the scribes), Jesus shows us his acute powers of observation. Here, too, we see the world through those same discerning eyes. The wealthy make their donations with an appropriate show, the widow rather cautiously, but we are then provided with Jesus' take on giving.

Jesus evaluates the level of generosity not so much by the fiscal value as by the spiritual cost. The widow has staked her all on God. Perhaps it is this, more than even the percentage amount of her gift compared with her total assets, that matters. She shows that she trusts God enough and desires him enough to invest everything she has in him. Regardless of the amounts the rich people give, they ensure that they are still in control. It is this widow's sense of complete dependence that Jesus is commending, and this is what lay behind his challenge to the rich ruler to give away everything. Jesus himself will face the same challenge in Gethsemane.

It is worth gathering together some other features that emerge from Jesus about giving. First there is the source of wealth: if riches come by 'devouring widows' houses' (20:47), they will not be approved by God. Equally, if the motive for giving is to receive human acclamation, the giver has already been rewarded and cannot expect recognition from God.

5 Apocalyptic warnings

Luke 21:12–19

Jesus could not allow people to invest their trust in the wrong things, whether it was their capacity to give because they were wealthy or the apparent glory of the temple in Jerusalem.

The status of the temple was disputed within Judaism. Whereas for some, as in the time of Jeremiah, the temple was their guarantee of God's protection and favour, for others (such as the Qumran community) it was an indication of apostasy.

The temple that stood before Jesus was the one that was in the process of being built by Herod (whose nationality was not 'pure' Jewish) over several decades. It is also the one whose foundation platform, known to us as the Western Wall, still generates such devotion today.

It is difficult to be sure that we have properly understood passages like Luke 21 (and Matthew 24 and Mark 13), which represent a genre of contemporary writing known as 'apocalyptic'. This is partly because it is difficult to know whether the referent (the event or the place being destroyed) is primarily a historical one or whether it is an apocalyptic symbol indicating a process that will lead eventually to the 'new age' that God will bring in.

What is clear in this presentation, however, is that Jesus did not paint these disturbing and fascinating pictures for their own sake. He was no science-fiction writer. His intention was not merely to predict the future but to provide support and guidance for the disciples, so that they would know what to do when these horrific events did eventually take place.

There are three main strands to Jesus' guidance. Firstly, the disciples are not to be misled by people's false claims, even if those claims are made in Jesus' name. Secondly, whatever terrible events do happen, they are not to be seen as indicating that God has lost control of the world or that he is no longer able to bring things to his desired conclusion—which will be the complete renewal of earth and heaven.

Thirdly (and this is the most important component of this section), the disciples personally will face serious trouble and need to be ready for it. Verse 12 is, in one sense, a summary of Acts, especially of Paul's experiences. All these difficulties will be 'an opportunity to testify' (v. 13), that is, to establish the validity of the Christian testimony to Jesus—which is what Luke's Gospel is doing. Just as Jesus can silence his opponents now, so he will enable his followers to do likewise by providing them with the necessary responses to their accusers. It is worth noting that Mark makes reference to the Holy Spirit in a similar passage (see Mark 13:11). Luke refers more often to the Holy Spirit than the other Gospels do.

It may seem rather strange, even contradictory, for Jesus to tell his disciples that some will be murdered (v. 16) 'but not a hair of your head will perish' (v. 18). This indicates further how difficult it is to be sure we have understood the implications of this 'apocalyptic' language exactly.

6 Cosmic chaos

Luke 21:20–38

This passage, with its description of the 'end times', moves through several phases. Starting with the destruction of Jerusalem (which was of theological as well as historical significance because of Jerusalem's symbolic role in scripture), it moves on to a set of cosmic events (vv. 25–27). The 'roaring of the sea and waves' might not seem 'cosmic' to us, but the psalms celebrating God's kingship (especially 93:3–4; 96:11, 13; 98:7–9) indicate that such phenomena were associated with God's dramatic intervention in creation. It is worth noting that even the sight of 'the Son of Man coming in a cloud' is only the prelude to 'redemption drawing near' (vv. 27–28) and all these events indicate only that 'the kingdom of God is near' (v. 31): neither redemption nor the kingdom has yet arrived. We could spend many sessions unravelling the background to every word here, but perhaps it is more important to focus on the purpose of Jesus in speaking these words.

Firstly, we can note Luke's stress on the physical context: Jesus is teaching in the temple (19:47; 20:1; 21:1, 5, 37–38). Jesus, the rejected stone, is witnessing against the temple, as the Lord who has come to the temple (see Malachi 3:1–3). It is perhaps in this context of a witness against the temple and Jerusalem that his claim in verse 33 should be heard. 'Heaven and earth' are summoned as witnesses to God's pronouncements in the Old Testament (see Deuteronomy 30:19; Isaiah 1:2; compare Isaiah 51:6).

Secondly (as we also noted in the previous reading), Jesus does not provide these graphic accounts to impress people with his predictive powers. Rather, his intention is to guide his followers and give them assurance in preparation for a dangerous and very frightening time. Verse 21 provides instructions for survival at the time of the sack of Jerusalem by the Romans. Verse 34 seeks to stimulate the proper Christian response during these 'testing times'. The disciples are not to be caught unawares (a concern expressed earlier, in 17:22–36), or absorbed in worldly ambitions or immoral practices. Rather, they are to develop proper spiritual disciplines—being alert and praying for 'strength to escape' (v. 36; compare the Lord's Prayer in Luke 11:4).

Thirdly, Jesus reassures his hearers that none of these apparently random, life-threatening and cosmically catastrophic events surprises or undermines him, so they shouldn't dissolve his disciples' faith, either. Indeed, his words will remain established as true even after the end of this age and into the age to come (v. 33). Each phase moves them nearer to his and their goal—the day of redemption or the establishment of God's kingdom. The great climax and, therefore, their aim must be 'to stand before the Son of Man' (v. 36).

So, as Luke prepares to take his readers through the horrors of Jesus' crucifixion, he does so by describing a cosmic chaos that they can survive, assuring them that Jesus is aware and in control. Just as Jesus will come through crucifixion into the resurrection, so he will bring his disciples through to the age to come.

Guidelines

In so many ways, Luke is heightening the tensions in the story he tells. The coming death of Jesus is not to be viewed as the death of a wandering Jewish teacher or of a kind and compassionate man who lived a good life, never harmed anyone and helped those who were distressed, poor or ill. No: the death of Jesus is the critical moment in Jewish history. Like an underwater earthquake, the shock waves it generates will eventually crash over Jerusalem and wipe it out. Throughout the aftershock of his death, life will be tough for the disciples, but they are neither to lose their confidence in him nor to be duped by false claims. Rather, they are to seek, through prayer, the clear-sightedness and strength that will enable them to continue as faithful disciples. There is much here to challenge us, even if we live with the receding waves and debris.

FURTHER READING

I. Howard Marshall, *The Gospel of Luke* (New International Greek Testament Commentary), Paternoster, 1978.

Darrell L. Bock, *Luke* (IVP New Testament Commentary), IVP, 1994.

Henry Wansbrough, *Luke* (People's Bible Commentary), BRF, 1998.

Tom Wright, *Luke for Everyone*, SPCK, 2001.

Jesus and leadership

In today's wide-ranging leadership debate, those who turn to Jesus for answers may at first be disappointed. Beyond the challenges not to lead like the Gentiles who 'lord it over' their subjects (Mark 10:42) and not to lead like the Pharisees who 'do not practise what they preach' (Matthew 23:3), there is precious little in the Gospels that specifically relates to a leadership theme. Indeed, Jesus seems to have actively discouraged his disciples from thinking of themselves as leaders (see Matthew 23:8–9), encouraging them to focus their attention instead on what it means to be followers, learners, servants and friends. John's Gospel, in particular, presents even Jesus as a disciple first (for example, 5:19; 8:26, 29; 12:49). What, then, can we learn about leadership from the perfect disciple?

Some years ago, I wrote a book entitled *The Fourfold Leadership of Jesus* (BRF, 2008), in which I drew out four words from the Gospels—Come, Follow, Wait and Go—to illustrate four aspects of Jesus' leadership: that it was accessible ('Come'), inspirational ('Follow'), long-term ('Wait') and missional ('Go'). I have now been invited to revisit these themes with some fresh thoughts and insights.

If we begin with Jesus' call to 'Come to me', we can imagine a leader—Jesus, no less—who is facing his followers, his arms outstretched in a gesture of warmth and welcome: 'Come to me' suggests an approach to leadership that has accessibility right at its core. It is gentle leadership, friendly and compassionate, calling others into a closeness of relationship that is both enriching and mutually exposing.

'Follow me' leadership is not so much accessible as inspirational. It speaks of integrity and courage, an ability to set a direction, then stick to it. On its own it can become relentless and tiring, with only the fittest keeping up and a trail of casualties falling by the wayside. But at its best—when combined with the warmer characteristics of 'Come to me' accessibility—it provides an excellent model of a leadership that is caring but not cosy, authoritative but not authoritarian, decisive but not driven.

Following Jesus, of course, is fundamental to any understanding of Christian discipleship, but Paul takes it one step further. If the world around us is to understand what following Jesus looks like today, ordinary Christian men and women need to embody that 'followership' themselves. Paul would have had no patience with the common sentiment, 'Don't follow me, follow Jesus'. His call was, rather, 'Follow my example, as I follow the example of Christ' (1 Corinthians 11:1).

1 Gentleness and humility

Matthew 11:25–30

From shepherds on the hillsides to wise men from the east; from prostitutes and tax collectors to Pharisees and teachers of the law; from respectable Jewish leaders who came to him by night to dodgy Samaritan women who met him in the heat of the day, the sheer variety of those who chose to respond to Jesus' invitation to 'Come to me' is remarkable. Other leaders in history may have gathered more followers in the course of their life on earth than Jesus did, but no one else has proved so variously magnetic to men and women, young and old, rich and poor, Jew and Gentile, 'establishment' and outcast alike.

What might account for the breadth of Jesus' appeal, which now spans the continents and makes him indisputably the most widely loved and revered leader of all time? Leaving aside for a moment the Christian claim that he was and is the Son of God, the sheer winsome accessibility of his 'Come to me' invitation is probably the key.

It was an invitation issued to 'all who are weary and burdened' (v. 28), in marked contrast to Jesus' devastating critique of the Pharisees of his day, who 'tie up heavy, cumbersome loads and put them on other people's shoulders, but they themselves are not willing to lift a finger to move them' (23:4). It was an invitation issued by a man who himself drew great joy and strength from the ready accessibility of his heavenly Father. At its heart lay an offer to his hearers to remove the 'heavy, cumbersome' yoke of the legalists and to take on the easy yoke of God's grace—the oppression of enslavement replaced by the refreshment of a happy marriage.

Two qualities in particular contribute to Jesus' 'Come to me' accessibility: humility and gentleness. Humility—the natural, unaffected interest in others that springs from a place of inner security rather than personal worthlessness—is a hugely attractive attribute; while gentleness (the Greek word literally means 'strength under control') enables leaders to be safely approachable without the attendant dangers of coercion, manipulation or seduction.

What is the source of humility and gentleness for us, as for Jesus? Simply this: the quality of our relationship with our 'Father, Lord of heaven and earth' (v. 25).

2 Compassion and vulnerability

Matthew 14:13–21

'Compassion' in modern English is a noun, something we have. *Splachnizomai* in New Testament Greek is a verb, something we do, and there's an important distinction between the two that goes way beyond mere semantics. In a world where we 'have' compassion, it's easy for pastors or their secular equivalents to assume that compassion simply goes with the job—that it's something fixed, framed and stuck to the wall along with the various degrees and other qualifications they have picked up along the way. But the verb *splanchnizomai* reminds us that such an approach is nonsense. 'Compassioning' in the biblical sense speaks of a gutsy involvement with another person (the Greek word *splanchna* means 'guts'), which is both passionate and practical. In John's stark words, 'Dear children, let us not love with words or tongue but with actions and in truth' (1 John 3:18).

Today's reading sees Jesus doing compassion on a grand scale. He has just returned from a 'solitary place' after hearing news of the murder of his friend and cousin John the Baptist (see 14:1–12). He may have been feeling vulnerable, the depth of his sense of loss exacerbated by fears for his own safety. Yet here before him is the largest crowd he has yet encountered—themselves confused and bewildered, 'like sheep without a shepherd' (Mark 6:34), now that Pastor John has met with such a sordid end. As Jesus looks out on them, he feels compassion, a gutsy self-giving love that finds expression in a series of healing miracles and (to borrow a detail from John 6:9) the dramatic multiplication of a boy's packed lunch.

A verse from the book of Ezekiel comes to mind—'I will remove from you your heart of stone and give you a heart of flesh' (Ezekiel 36:26)—for nothing short of a divinely initiated heart transplant is required to set us free from self-absorption and release us into compassioning. Christian experience teaches that such a transplant is not just a one-off event: *splanchnizomai* is rather to be a daily commitment, lived out of the freshness of encounter with a God whose love is 'new every morning' (Lamentations 3:23).

3 The good doctor

Matthew 9:9–17

There are various touching images of 'Come to me' leadership in the Gospels: the good shepherd, who 'calls his own sheep by name', who knows his own and is known by them (John 10:3, 14); the good father, who has compassion on his wretched son 'while he was still a long way off' and runs to welcome him home (Luke 15:20); even the good chicken who 'gathers her chicks under her wings' (Luke 13:34)—a remarkably feminine picture of Jesus' desire to draw the people of Jerusalem around himself. Humility, gentleness, vulnerability and compassion are embodied in each of these images, along with the gathering instinct that brings people together for encouragement and protection.

Perhaps the most straightforward of all the 'Come to me' images, though (certainly for today's urban dwellers, whose understanding of the ways of sheep and chickens is often rather patchy) is that of the good doctor in today's reading. Jesus is being criticised, as so often, for the company he keeps. His decision to call Matthew has only made matters worse, as a great company of tax collectors and unspecified 'sinners' has decided to join the party. Even John the Baptist's disciples come close to allying themselves with the Pharisees in their confusion at Jesus' unorthodox approach. In this potentially explosive situation, Jesus makes the simplest of observations: 'It is not the healthy who need a doctor, but those who are ill' (v. 12).

It's simple but brilliant. In one small sentence Jesus outlines exactly what his ministry is about, and why accessibility lies at its heart. Doctors are there for the sick. Doctors are accessible. The idea of a doctor who shudders every time a sick person walks into the surgery, constantly keeps patients at arm's length or responds to the sight of a tumour with undisguised disgust is ridiculous. Yet such, implies Jesus, is the philosophy of the Pharisees; and such remains the philosophy of all those today who allow sacrifice—whether of a ritualistic or self-disciplined variety—to override their commitment to mercy (v. 13; see Hosea 6:6, from which Jesus quotes).

In the famous words of Paul from 1 Corinthians 13:3, 'If I give all I possess to the poor and give over my body to the flames, but have not love, I gain nothing.'

4 Life on the pedestal

Matthew 23:1–12

Pedestals come in all shapes and sizes. They can be self-built or constructed by others on their hero's behalf. They are variously welcomed or resented by those who are placed upon them. They leave their subjects isolated, vulnerable to a host of leadership temptations and precariously defenceless in response to the fickle winds of public opinion. They fatally undermine any attempt at 'Come to me' leadership.

We can witness, in Jesus' day, a number of people apparently relishing the pedestals on which they were set—Caesar Augustus in far-off Rome, for example, together with other, lesser 'rulers of the Gentiles' and their 'high officials', whose leadership style was both authoritarian and detached (see Mark 10:42).

Jesus' main concern, though, was not so much the power pedestal as what we might call the 'righteousness pedestal'. This is the tendency among religious people to claim the moral high ground—even to become nakedly competitive—on the basis of their dedication, discipline, obedience and sheer hard work. It's not that there's anything wrong with dedication, discipline, obedience and sheer hard work, of course: it is qualities like these that characterise every leader of genuine spiritual stature. But if the motivation is wrong—if 'everything is done for people to see' (v. 5)—these good materials become worthless or worse. Pedestal-building or character-building? That is the choice that Jesus sets before us, and it's impossible to do both at the same time.

The materials from which the Pharisees' pedestals were constructed are clearly set out in Matthew 23. They included elaborate dressing-up, impressive titles, a consistent emphasis on the externals of religion and a claim to the best seat in the house (most of them rather uncomfortable areas for bishops like myself!)—to which we might add showy prayers, ostentatious fasting and maximum publicity when it came to giving to the needy (see Matthew 6:1–2), along with countless examples of keeping sinners at arm's length.

Lest we should be tempted to say, 'Thank you, Lord, that I am not like that Pharisee', though, a little humility—indeed, a sustained period of self-examination—is undoubtedly required. What is my pedestal? Who's building it? How does it distance me from others? How might it be cut down to size? These are questions that every Christian leader needs to be asking on a pretty regular basis.

We are, after all, followers of the one who, 'being in very nature God… made himself nothing, taking the very nature of a servant' (Philippians 2:6–7).

5 The changing room

Exodus 33:7–11

The apostle Paul's instruction to the church in Colosse, that as 'God's chosen people, holy and dearly loved' they were to 'clothe [them]selves with compassion, kindness, humility, gentleness and patience' (Colossians 3:12), suggests that the qualities of the 'Come to me' leader should permeate the whole church. Indeed, it doesn't take long for most church congregations to begin to share the strengths and emphases (and weaknesses and prejudices) of those who lead them—a distinctly alarming thought for all who are called to this most responsible of ministries.

But if we are to clothe ourselves, where is the changing room?

Our readings so far have already hinted at the need for 'Come to me' leaders to draw strength from time alone with their heavenly Father. For Jesus, this was the 'solitary place' from which he emerged to do compassion on a grand scale (Matthew 14:13–14); in today's reading it is the 'tent of meeting' where 'the Lord would speak to Moses face to face, as one speaks to a friend' (v. 11). Finding our tent or solitary place—entering into God's presence as his 'chosen people, holy and dearly loved'—helps to remind us of who we are and what we're called to do, and to put in perspective the myriad concerns and preoccupations that all too frequently keep others at arm's length. Accessibility (ironically) depends on times of inaccessibility. In order to advance, we need first to retreat. Regular access to the Father is essential for all who would be accessible to his children.

Moses' own accessibility, of course, was legendary, as befits a 'very humble man, more humble than anyone else on the face of the earth' (Numbers 12:3). No one could accuse Moses of pedestal-building during his lifetime, and even in his death this remarkable man of God was buried in an unmarked grave (Deuteronomy 34:6). There is one incident that perhaps reminds us of the dark side of accessibility—the sense that 'it all depends on me'—and here the advice of father-in-law Jethro played an important part in Moses' education (see Exodus 18:13–23). Proper leadership structures should complement, not compete with, the godly desire to be accessible to others. Such was the essence of Jethro's approach, and today's 'Come to me' leaders ignore Jethro at their peril.

The central point remains, though: where is my changing room, and when did I last pay it a visit?

6 The accessible church

1 Corinthians 14:1–25

Paul's teaching about the role of prophecy and tongues in public worship might not seem an obvious place to conclude our 'Come to me' reflections, but there are certain principles in this chapter that are relevant to every church with a vision to reach out to the community it serves.

The first principle (following on from 1 Corinthians 13) is to 'pursue love' (v. 1, NRSV)—the kind of gentle, compassionate, impartial love that was the hallmark of Jesus' own ministry. Here we are reminded of James' satirical picture of a church that is all too welcoming to the rich man (whose tithe would come in very handy) while horribly dismissive of the vagrant (the state of whose personal hygiene spells trouble) (James 2:1–7). Beware, says James, of such acts of blatant discrimination.

But a church may be loving, yet not comprehensible: welcoming at the front door but quietly excluding the spiritually uneducated or inexperienced when they step inside. Hence Paul's concerns about the unregulated use of the gift of tongues in worship, which so excludes the enquirer or unbeliever (vv. 16, 23). The church in Corinth would probably have described itself as a 'welcoming church' (almost every church does). It was certainly pretty lively. But Paul put his finger on an area where the Corinthians' undoubted enthusiasm was making God inaccessible to all but the initiated. Complicated preaching, turgid liturgy and incomprehensible hymns can do the same in other contexts.

It's possible, though, for a church to work so hard to be user-friendly that it becomes mundane and stodgy, with no real expectancy of the Spirit of God at work, and such a picture was far from Paul's mind. In whatever way we interpret the New Testament gift of prophecy, Paul's vision was of a church that genuinely connected newcomers to the living God (v. 25). An accessible welcome and comprehensible language might be all very well, but the heart of the church's calling is to live out the truth of Ephesians 2:18, that 'through [Christ] we… have access to the Father by one Spirit'.

'I don't go to church because I'm not good enough'; 'I don't go to church because I wouldn't know what to do'; 'I don't go to church because it's boring.' These remain among the biggest obstacles to people in responding positively to the church's invitation, 'Come to me'. Only a church that is welcoming, comprehensible and genuinely spiritual will remove those obstacles and draw others into the arms of their humble and gentle Saviour.

Guidelines

The sheer accessibility of Jesus' approach to leadership throws up many questions and challenges for all who would model their leadership on his. But the first step is very simple: our job is to draw close to the Father. Everything else flows from that.

As we focus on Jesus' 'Come to me' leadership, we might pray:

- for a freshness and discipline in our own response to the call of Jesus to 'come to me'.
- for God to clothe us afresh with the qualities of gentleness, humility and compassion.
- for wisdom to discern the pedestals that we build for ourselves or allow others to build for us.
- for our churches to become places of genuine welcome to those on or beyond the fringe.

Finally, here are some words for reflection from Horatio Bonar:

I heard the voice of Jesus say,
'Come unto me and rest;
lay down, thou weary one, lay down
thy head upon my breast.'
I came to Jesus as I was,
so weary, worn and sad;
I found in him a resting place,
and he has made me glad.

1 Authority and insight

Mark 1:16–28

In an age when choice is king, it is both surprising and reassuring to be reminded that we are chosen—that, in Jesus' own words, 'You did not choose me, but I chose you' (John 15:16). In Jesus' day, as in our own, there was a kind of 'buyer's market' when it came to choosing a rabbi. You could shop around to find a religious leader whose teaching made sense, just as many people today shop around for a guru or life-coach, or travel from church to church in a quest to find the preacher or pastor of their choice. There is nothing new in a consumerist approach to religion.

Jesus was different: in the terms of my analogy, Jesus acted as if it were a seller's market. Nowhere is that clearer than in the rollercoaster opening chapter of Mark's Gospel and in Jesus' call to four fishermen to 'Follow me'.

What, then, gave Jesus the authority to behave in such an unusually directive way—an authority that was rapidly being gossiped about in the synagogue in Capernaum and throughout the surrounding countryside? It came in part from a radical simplicity of approach, which contrasted with the tiresome nitpicking of the scribes and Pharisees, and in part from Jesus' intimate connectedness with the power of the living God. Jesus bursts on to the scene in Mark 1 much as David bursts on to the scene in 1 Samuel 16 and 17. Both David and 'King David's greater son' were far bigger than their contemporaries in terms of their clarity of vision and the decisiveness that went with it.

It's one thing, though, to have clarity of vision and quite another to help others to find their part within that vision, and this is where the second part of Jesus' call—'Follow me and I will make you fish for people'—is so striking. We might want to emphasise here the uniquely life-giving nature of such a fishing trip, but the essence of what Jesus is saying is clear. 'I can take the gifts and experience you have, the skills and courage required in tracking down fish, and I can help you use them to fulfil God's purposes into all eternity.'

This reminds us again of Jesus' words in John 15:16: 'You did not choose me, but I chose you and appointed you so that you might go and bear fruit—fruit that will last.' It's no wonder that 'at once they left their nets and followed him' (Mark 1:18).

2 Integrity and sacrifice

John 13:1–15

It was both conscious and deliberate—Jesus' response to a social gaffe which had left his disciples both wrong-footed and dirty-footed! John's Gospel largely shields us from the tensions developing around this time as the disciples increasingly jostled for position in preparation for the glory they believed to be imminent. But the sight of a rabbi—especially *this* rabbi—bending down and washing the feet of the Twelve still holds up an uncomfortable mirror to our human condition, and especially to the perils of the pecking order.

The shame of stepping out of line, breaking a social taboo or potentially demeaning ourselves before our peers is often a far more powerful force in people's lives than guilt at disobeying even the most fundamental of God's laws. According to this philosophy, the greatest sin of all is to get caught in the act, with all the publicity and embarrassment that follows. Religious people, especially religious leaders, are certainly not immune from such a distorted perspective—quite the reverse, in fact, as we've been reminded in our earlier reflections on the building of pedestals.

Elsewhere in the Gospels, Jesus commends a variety of (often) unlikely role models for others to follow—destitute widows, little children, Samaritan lepers, Roman soldiers and notorious 'sinners' among them—but here he deliberately points to his own actions as an example to his disciples. Here is someone who doesn't just see the big picture, but lives it. His inner security is so well rooted that talk of 'pecking orders' is entirely out of place: he is (to use Os Guinness' telling phrase) 'playing to an audience of One'. There's integrity here, and courage, as well as a foretaste of the sacrifice to come—as the Greek phrase for 'taking off' his outer robe (v. 4) is not new to readers of John's Gospel. It has already been used of the good shepherd, who 'lays down' his life for the sheep (10:11).

How, then, were the disciples to follow Jesus' example, and so to become models for others to follow? Yes, by giving, but also by being humble enough to receive. Before Jesus washed his disciples' feet, he himself had his feet anointed with costly oil (John 12:3), and the same principle must apply to his followers, Simon Peter first among them.

'Freely you have received' is the root of all true 'Follow me' leadership. 'Freely give' is its fruit.

3 The pioneer and perfecter

Hebrews 12:1–3

While Jesus used a number of images, the doctor and the good shepherd among them, to illustrate his 'Come to me' leadership, it's up to the author of the letter to the Hebrews to give us the best illustration of the

'Follow me' leader. The Greek terms *archegos* and *teleiotes* are not found elsewhere in the New Testament, although they relate to the description of Jesus as the 'Beginning [*arche*] and the End [*telos*]' in Revelation 22:13. Yet the call to 'run with perseverance the race that is set before us, looking to Jesus, the pioneer [*archegos*] and perfecter [*teleiotes*] of our faith' (v. 2, RSV) remains a rich and stirring image.

Pioneers are clear-sighted, boldly going where no one has gone before. They speak with authority, seeing to the heart of an issue and refusing to be tied down by the hundred-and-one petty conventions of their lesser contemporaries. They are more concerned with 'doing the right thing' than with 'doing things right'. Theirs is a proactive approach to living, contrasting sharply with the cautious, defensive approach of other people around them.

When faced, say, with the decision of whether or not to heal on the sabbath (see Matthew 12:10) or how to respond to a woman caught in the act of adultery (John 8:5), pioneers will instinctively know the best course to follow, whatever the booby traps along the way. The very boldness with which they approach such issues, though, will delight some while leaving others confused, wrong-footed and sometimes very angry (Matthew 12:14).

Perfecters, on the other hand, are those who see the job through, who frequently pick up where the pioneers leave off, bringing to the party the dogged perseverance of the completer-finisher. In Genesis 1 we read of God himself as both pioneer and perfecter, the one who initiates and the one who completes: 'In the beginning God created the heavens and the earth... By the seventh day God had finished the work he had been doing' (1:1; 2:2). In John's Gospel we read the same of Jesus, the Word of God who was 'with God in the beginning' (1:2) and whose final cry from the cross was the triumphant 'It is finished' (19:30).

While pioneers can be dangerous and perfecters dull, a perfect pioneer provides the best possible role model for us to follow.

4 Blindness and hypocrisy

Matthew 23:13–28

The most useful guide on any walking or climbing expedition is one who has excellent eyesight and knows the terrain well. The least useful is one whose eyesight is poor and has never been that way before. That, in essence, is Jesus' charge against the Pharisees in the second half of Matthew 23, to add to the charge of pedestal-building in the first half: they were blind guides and hypocrites, who had never entered the holiness terrain they were seeking to inflict on others.

Every culture, of course, has its blind spots—its unique combination of conventions and traditions, emphases and prejudices, which mark it out from the cultures around it. Whenever two cultures come together (as, say, on a wedding day), it's not long before the peculiarities of each are exposed to the other. Whether it's little words or phrases that have become part of the family vocabulary or more serious issues like our attitudes to money or communication, that exposure is variously funny, embarrassing and illuminating. At worst it leads to relationship meltdown; at best it brings a greater self-knowledge and (for the Christian) a clearer assessment of how many of our values are cultural and how many are genuinely rooted in the soil of the gospel.

The clash of cultures between Jesus and the Pharisees could hardly have been revealed more clearly than in Matthew 23. The description of spiritual tunnel-vision that ignores matters of justice, mercy and faithfulness while simultaneously insisting that the tiny leaves on every mint bush should be counted and tithed may have been a parody, but it illustrates an approach to holiness that, in Jesus' understanding, completely missed the mark.

Worse than their cultural blind spots, though, were the examples of hypocrisy that marred the Pharisees' record and entirely disqualified them as 'Follow me' leaders: in Jesus' famous summary, 'Do not do what they do, because they do not practise what they preach' (Matthew 23:3). It seems that, at times, the religious act was so convincing that even the actors themselves were taken in.

The message for all would-be inspirational leaders is clear: it is not that we have to be entirely clear-sighted and perfect in every way (only Jesus, the 'pioneer and perfecter', is that), but that we need to be fearless in our cultivation of a spirit of honesty, humility and self-knowledge. Otherwise, the only place we will lead others is up the garden path.

5 Tablets and pillars

Exodus 33:12—34:4

Obedience is hardly a fashionable virtue outside the walls of religious orders and the ranks of the armed services. The idea that one person has the authority to tell another person what to do or how to behave is increasingly challenged in an age when there is much talk of rights and little talk of responsibilities. Even in church circles, an undue emphasis on God's unconditional love can all too easily leave obedience out in the cold. Some preaching gets alarmingly close to the theology caricatured by Paul in Romans 6:1: 'Keep on sinning so that God can keep on forgiving' (THE MESSAGE).

Obedience, though, lies at the heart of our covenant relationship with God, as an expression of our gratitude to him for calling us into that relationship in the first place. In the story of the exodus, obedience is symbolised by the tablets of stone and the pillars of cloud and fire (see Exodus 13:21)—by the word of God and the presence of God with his people. In the Gospel story, it is focused on Jesus (himself both the Word of God and presence of God), who neatly brings together the themes of love and obedience in John 15:10: 'If you keep my commands, you will remain in my love, just as I have kept my Father's commands and remain in his love.'

The last part of that verse is especially significant, for it reminds us that Jesus' authority as a 'Follow me' leader is directly related to his obedience as a 'Follow God' disciple. The same was true for Moses as he contemplated the awesome task that lay before him, and the same is true for us. If we are to avoid the spiritual blindness and hypocrisy of the Pharisees, if we are to be role models for others to follow (and how desperately the world needs such role models), and if we are to live lives of authority and integrity, we must attend to the tablets and the pillars—to pray daily for obedience to the word of God and openness to the presence of God.

Without obedience we become flabby and weak-willed; without openness, judgmental and hard-hearted.

6 The inspirational church

2 Corinthians 8:1–7

The congregations in Macedonia, Smyrna and Philadelphia were not obvious contenders for the annual 'Church of the Year' award. They were small, poor, embattled and far less flourishing than their counterparts in Ephesus, Corinth and Laodicea.

The congregations in Macedonia, Smyrna and Philadelphia had one thing in common, though, alongside their poverty and smallness: each one was held up as a model for others to follow. Smyrna and Philadelphia were the only two churches given a clean bill of health by the risen Jesus in Revelation 2—3, while the Macedonian Christians were applauded by Paul for their overflowing joy and their rich generosity.

There is a link between today's reading and the ethos of the Gospels, where (as we have seen) Jesus frequently picked out a quality in an unlikely individual and held it up for others to emulate. Jesus was more generous than we are in this regard: his role models were not all-rounders when it came to faith and virtue, but were specialists. The Roman centurion, for example, was applauded for the directness of his faith; the Samaritan leper was blessed for returning to say 'thank you'; the prostitute was honoured for the depth of her love.

The most obvious parallel here, though, is the story of the widow's mite—the two small coins that she placed in the temple treasury, representing 'all she had to live on' (Luke 21:4). Like the churches in Macedonia, who combined extreme poverty with rich generosity, the extent of that woman's sacrifice will always serve as a vivid challenge to those who have more and give less.

So will the search for inspiration always lead us to the small, the poor and the embattled? Not necessarily, although the scriptures suggest that they are good places to start. Our natural tendency is to be like the prophet Samuel, who began with the big and impressive and only reluctantly made his way down to the shepherd boy who was ruddy, handsome and alarmingly immature (1 Samuel 16). The words spoken by the Lord on that occasion retain their relevance for those who are seeking inspiration, role models and godly 'Follow me' leadership: 'People look at the outward appearance, but the Lord looks at the heart' (v. 7).

Guidelines

The challenge of our readings this week applies to every disciple of Christ. All of us are called to be the salt of the earth and the light of the world, and, in that sense, to be role models in our families, workplaces, churches and communities. At the heart of this calling is the joyful obedience that springs from a place of gratitude and love.

As we focus on Jesus' 'Follow me' leadership, we might pray:

- for a willingness to give God fresh authority in our lives, rather than treating his word as a kind of 'pick-and-mix' offering.
- for a fresh ability to see clearly, to live what we see and to help others discern their own part in the purposes of God.
- for ourselves and our churches to become role models for others through the presence of God's Spirit within us, living out the life of the gospel in ways that are countercultural, attractive and inspiring.

Here are some words of reflection from John Greenleaf Whittier:

> In simple trust like theirs who heard,
> beside the Syrian sea,
> the gracious calling of the Lord,
> let us, like them, without a word,
> rise up and follow thee.

The fruit of the Spirit

In season and out of season we can enjoy a rich variety of fruit, which we know is good for our physical health and well-being. The fruit we will consider over the next two weeks is the fruit of the Spirit, intended for our spiritual health and well-being. We can pick and choose from the variety of fruit on sale in the shops, with its amazing array of colours and countries of origin, but the fruit of the Spirit comes together as a complete bowlful, which is to be found and expressed through our Christian pilgrimage.

Paul writes of the fruit of the Spirit in his letter to the Galatians (5:22–23), after first speaking of the works of the flesh (vv. 19–21). These works of the flesh could be described as the shadow side, a part of the negativity that at times envelops our being, emphasising our weaknesses rather than our giftedness.

We shall look at the fruit of the Spirit from a positive perspective, albeit acknowledging the shadows as well. For many people, their limitations and weaknesses are easier to name than the things they are good at doing and enjoy in life. In acknowledging our limitations and weaknesses, we may learn more about our giftedness, and through it all the rich variety of the fruit of the Spirit will be revealed to us.

There is a saying, 'No pain, no gain'. I'm not sure I agree totally with that, as it depends on how we interpret the word 'pain' and understand the word 'gain'. Yet, it is sometimes through the difficult and painful experiences of life that we become more aware of the fruit of the Spirit; then we may rejoice in these expressions of God, seeded within us and blossoming into maturity.

All biblical quotations are taken from the New Revised Standard Version.

5–11 August

1 Love (I)

1 John 4:7–21

The various forms of the fruit of the Spirit come out from, and culminate in, love—the greatest of them all (1 Corinthians 13:13). They are embraced in love and are revealed in and through love. This is a love that comes through the faith we have; this is a love that is perfected in us by God (1 John 4:12).

What do we mean by love? Individuals may have experiences of so-called 'love' within their lives that are degrading and abusive rather than empowering or enabling—expressions of selfishness, not the fruit of the Spirit. As the Greeks understood, though, with their various words for it, true love can be expressed in many ways and can mean many things, and within the Bible we discover those different aspects of love. Love may be found in friendship (*philia*), as in the relationship between David and Jonathan (1 Samuel 18:1); it may be sensual (*eros*), as described in the Song of Songs; and it may be unconditional and self-sacrificial (*agape*), as seen in the life and death of Jesus. As Julian of Norwich wrote in her *Revelations of Divine Love*, the whole meaning of all that Jesus did for us was love, and this is the love that John is writing about in our passage today (vv. 9–10).

As we read in this passage, our loving finds its birth within the love of God, 'for God is love' (v. 8) and 'we love because he first loved us' (v. 19). Flowing from that love is the call in faith that 'those who love God must love their brothers and sisters also' (v. 21).

Love grows up through trusting and knowing someone (see vv. 7–8). To know the love of God means that we must get to know God within the context of our lives and must pass God's love on to others (v. 11). It also means coming to know our own self, and to love our self as we are loved by God. To follow the way of love can at first lead us on an uncomfortable journey of self-knowledge and self-acceptance (see 1:8–9).

How easy is it to accept the love of God and to share that love with others? How do your own loving relationships with friends, family and others affect and reflect your relationship with God?

2 Joy

Luke 15:11–32

In this familiar parable, there are many layers of meaning to be un-ravelled, through which we can discover something more about God and our self. At times, when a passage or a parable is very well known, we can miss some of the subtle depths and nuances that open the door towards a deeper awareness and understanding of God.

The fruit of the Spirit we are considering today is joy. At first it would seem that, within this parable, there is a greater sense of self-indulgence (in the younger son), self-pity (the older son), and sorrow (the father) than there is of joy. Yet joy appears at the end, when the younger son returns home and is reunited with his family. The celebration that takes place is an expression of relief and an overflowing of love and joy. It is a dramatic illustration of the 'joy in heaven over one sinner who repents' that is described earlier in Luke 15, at the end of the parables of the lost sheep and the lost coin (see vv. 7, 10). A similar joy is found in the Old Testament prophecies of return from exile—for example, in Isaiah 35:10: 'And the ransomed of the Lord shall return, and come to Zion with singing; everlasting joy shall be upon their heads.'

Return, repentance, reconciliation: these are causes for joy in heaven, a joy that we may share, since the reconciling God has 'given us the ministry of reconciliation' (2 Corinthians 5:18). John of the Cross wrote that God would give us more joy if only we knew what to do with it! The elder son wasn't ready to know what to do with the joyful return of his brother, but the father did know what to do. Joy, in the parable and in our own everyday lives, can be found and celebrated in reconciliation between family members, which spreads out to embrace the wider community. This is a joy that gives a deep sense of well-being, of true contentment felt as a sustaining strength within.

How do you experience the joy of reconciliation in your life? What does 'joy' mean to you in a more general sense? Where may you find the experience of joy during this day?

3 Peace

Isaiah 32:14–20; 54:9–10

Within both these passages from Isaiah is the proclamation of God's desire for peace among his people and within creation. It brings us a sense of peace and hope when we see the fruitfulness of creation as a picture of the Spirit's blessing on us (32:15).

Peace is a fragile fruit, and, for many people within the present world, it is not a reality in their daily life. Images from our TV screens and newspapers reveal the truth that international peace is often torn apart by conflict, fear and warfare. Peace may not be a reality for us in our everyday experience, due to ill health, family commitments, restricted finances, fear of job loss, and the strains and stresses of modern life. Yet God's promise is that, amid the turmoil, though 'the mountains may depart and the hills be removed' (Isaiah 54:10), his covenant of peace will remain. So where and how can peace be offered?

A kind of 'peace' can be brought about by coercion: we might think of the *Pax Romana* in Jesus' day, or the 'peace walls' that divide warring communities in our own time. A true and lasting, fruitful peace, however, needs to come from the heart. Peace needs to evolve out of humanity's desire and love for all creation.

The Hebrew word for 'peace' is *shalom*, which opens up a wider definition than we usually understand by the word. *Shalom* incorporates a sense of wholeness and integrity that embraces a search for righteousness and justice, all of which are important elements of peace (see 32:16). *Shalom* is the peace that is to be sought within the community of the church, as well as within the wider community in which we live. This peace is accepting and supportive; it involves caring for and listening to those who share our lives in many and varied ways.

Jesus is the one who brings us peace through the Spirit (John 14:26–27), enabling us to be channels of God's peace wherever we are. To share that peace with others, first it is necessary to know it for ourselves. To bring the fruit of peace to the outer world, we need to feel it deep within us.

Have you sensed God's peace within you? Where and how do you find peace in your life? What are your concerns about peace within the world, within the place where you live, and within the church you belong to?

4 Patience

Matthew 13:1–9, 18–23

'Please, Lord, give me patience, and give it to me now' is a short arrow prayer that most of us will have thought of saying at some time or other. Patience is one fruit of the Spirit that we may find difficult to achieve—especially, perhaps, when it is most needed!

The world of today is characterised by speed. We expect to have everything now, instantly. Email and text messages have taken over from the slower communication method of sending a letter. 'Text-speak' shortens words to the minimum to make them quicker to type and send—although, ironically, it can test the patience of the reader in trying to make sense of the message. Television and other media bring us images from across the world as they are happening. While we may not want to be without this technology, it can often feel as if, instead of walking, the pace of life is more like a 100-metre sprint.

This raises the question of what is meant by the word 'patience'. Children in a school assembly, when asked, said that patience meant waiting. Waiting is one of the elements within patience; we could also include watching, resting, seeking, discerning, anticipating and hoping. In the parable in Matthew 13, the sower scatters the seed far and wide without looking to see whether it has fallen on good or bad soil. He will then need patience to watch over the crop as it grows, taking care especially of all that is growing to maturity (see James 5:7–8). Likewise, it takes time and patience to ensure that what we 'sow' or has been 'sown' in us by God comes to fruit a hundredfold.

To rush on without a patient waiting and watching may mean that we miss out on something special in our lives. Perhaps we miss seeing the changing colours and beauty of each passing season: life passes us by and we don't notice.

In our prayer, too, patience is needed. At times we may offer a quick arrow or shopping-list prayer, but we need also to rest in God, watching and waiting for the movement of the Spirit within. Without patience, we may miss God's call to us.

Where is patience needed in your life? How easy or difficult is it to have the patience to rest in prayer with God?

5 Kindness

Luke 6:31–42

Is kindness the hidden fruit of the Spirit? Perhaps it is not as obvious as some of the other fruits because of the quiet ways in which kindness is often shown and received. It is said that actions speak louder than words, and it is probably through our actions rather than our speech that kindness to another person is shown. The media rarely report acts of kindness, but occasionally we read of them—times when an anonymous person unexpectedly comes to the aid of someone in need. Those who receive such acts of kindness are likely to tell the story only to family or friends, if they mention it at all.

Kindness is closely connected to friendship and love—treating others as we ourselves would like to be treated (v. 31; see Matthew 22:39). As Christians, we are called through faith to imitate the way of God in our lives—a God who is kind and merciful even to 'the ungrateful and the wicked' (vv. 35–36). To offer kindness, then, means not being judgmental in our attitudes to others (v. 37); it means taking the 'log' out of our own eye first (v. 42). Kindness leads us to accept the other, looking beyond the surface to the real person beneath. It requires us to give without expecting any return (v. 35). Kindness is a fruit of the Spirit that should simply flow from us in love.

How does kindness affect us? It is unlikely that we consciously think, 'I have just offered an act of kindness'! More probably, we offer kindness because it is a part of who we are through our Christian faith and belief in God. We may never think very deeply about the kindness we give, but what does it feel like to be the one to receive an act of kindness by someone known or unknown?

To offer kindness, we need to learn how to be kind to ourselves, yet this may prove more difficult than being kind to someone else. Are you kind to yourself? How do you care for your own well-being, especially if you have many responsibilities and commitments in daily life? How has someone else offered you an act of kindness?

6 Love (II)

From kindness we come once again to love. Like kindness, love also means accepting another, looking beyond and beneath the surface to the person they truly are, the person they are called to be, by God.

The Song of Songs, or the Song of Solomon, is rarely heard in church, except perhaps when a few lines are read at a wedding. It is a piece of sensuous, erotic poetry, attempting to put into words the love felt between two people. The book may be interpreted as revealing not only this love between people, but also something of the loving relationship that God has with the church.

This may be a style of writing that makes us feel uncomfortable. If so, it raises the question of why we feel this way. Words of love between two people are usually kept private, unless they are partly shared with close family or friends. What words and expressions of love, though, are used as part of our conversation with the Divine, when we are in church?

Mystics as John of the Cross (1542–91) and Richard Rolle (c.1300–49) were very comfortable using the language of love when speaking about God and their relationship with God. It was their way of expressing how they felt, a way of putting into words all that they had experienced of God in their lives.

Following the pattern in the Song of Songs, John of the Cross wrote *The Spiritual Canticle*, which is a conversation between the soul (the bride) and the bridegroom. In *The Fire of Love*, Richard Rolle writes of the sensation felt within his soul, as though it were on fire with the love that he felt for God and God's love for him. In the book, Rolle writes out of his personal spiritual experiences, and there is a sense of a total giving of the self in love to God.

What words and phrases would you use to describe your relationship with God? Would you feel comfortable writing in the evocative style of the Song of Songs and the mystics? Do you think there is a need to be more open and expressive when speaking of our encounters with God in prayer?

Guidelines

This week we have looked at some of the fruit of the Spirit that Paul lists in Galatians 5—love, joy, peace, patience and kindness. These fruits all have the potential to be life-giving and life-enhancing. They feed into the creativity of the person we are, and reveal something of the Spirit dwelling within us.

Of the fruit we have considered this week, which one do you need most in your life today, and which one may you be able to offer to another person?

> Weave around us, O God, your patience,
> so we may rest in you and know your peace;
> through your peace may your kindness flow,
> and from that kindness may joy fill our lives.
> Embrace it all, in the strength
> and the gift of your love. Amen

12–18 August

1 Generosity

Acts 2:43–47

What does it mean to offer generosity or to be generous? Like the other fruit of the Spirit, generosity can reveal many layers of meaning. It connects us to the other fruit, such as love and kindness, in that to be generous of heart may require us to walk the extra mile in the giving of our time, to offer more of our self in service or to help someone financially. Generosity calls us to offer whatever we can, willingly, and with the desire to give something for no return, simply for the enablement of another.

In today's busy world, it may not be easy to be generous. Our time is precious, especially the time we spend with family and friends. Our money has to spread itself much further than it did before. There is a multitude of charities that we can support by giving our time or money: how do we choose which one or ones to support, without feeling ungenerous and guilty about those we cannot support?

In our reading from Acts 2, we discover a community of believers where all is held in common, all is shared. Today we may see that way of life only within a religious community or commune. Living as most of us do, it wouldn't be practical for us. Yet, there are many things we are to hold in common with all those who gather within our local community of believers. Faith calls us to be generous givers, to share what we can out of the resources that we have. We share in prayer and fellowship in worship; we may offer the hospitality of our home to group meetings. We share our gifts of building maintenance, cake making or organisational skills with the wider church community. To be generous means that we do not keep to ourselves the blessings we have been given.

Generosity is a fruit that needs to mature within us—to be offered out of love for God and from the faith we have, rather than out of the hope of reward from other people.

Thinking about the church you belong to, how is generosity shown within its life and mission? How generous a person do you feel you are? Are there ways in which you can share your own giftedness more generously within the church community?

2 Faithfulness

Genesis 9:8–17

This story of Noah is very familiar. Noah is faithful, so God returns that faithfulness by setting up a covenant relationship. This is a faithfulness that involves a two-way relationship—God to humanity and humanity to God. When we see the rainbow, it is a sign of wonder and beauty, bringing light to a darkened and rainy sky. The rainbow can also symbolise remembrance and hope, along with the fruit of faithfulness.

Faithfulness is related to commitment. The words have similar but slightly different meanings. The *Universal Dictionary* (Reader's Digest, 1994) describes commitment as making a pledge or promise to do something, or being bound to a person, cause or belief system, emotionally and/or intellectually. Faithfulness means being dutiful or loyal, and trusting a person, cause or belief system, so there is an overlap between these two ideas. Christian faith asks us both to be faithful and to have commitment—to do all that we say we will do.

To be faithful to God may, at times, be very easy: our faith is sure and certain, we are committed to the church we belong to, and we ensure that we are generous in all we offer. At other times, when life throws a boulder in our way or we fall into a pot-hole, hanging on to our faith, and being faithful, can be very difficult. In the good times, we do not need to see the symbolic rainbow in the sky, as we 'see' it in our hearts. In the not-so-good times, we may seek desperately for a glimpse of its colours, yet it seems to be covered by clouds; our true faithfulness and commitment may also seem covered by the dark, rainy skies. At those times, others may hold on to the hope of the rainbow for us.

Faithfulness is the call to be true to the person we are and are known to be by God. It requires us to acknowledge our limitations, to seek help if necessary, and to be generous in giving all that we are able to give.

To be faithful is to hear and follow the call of God and God's love—not necessarily having to build an ark, but simply to build within the context of our daily lives. What does it mean to you to be faithful?

3 Gentleness

1 Thessalonians 2:1–12; Matthew 11:28–30
When trying to understand what gentleness means, we can look at it from two perspectives—being gentle with other people and being gentle with ourselves. Paul and Jesus provide models for us to follow in developing both these aspects of gentleness.

As Paul shows us in the way he dealt with opposition, gentleness does not mean being afraid to speak one's mind, or complying with the will of others (1 Thessalonians 1:2, 4). Instead, gentleness takes into itself all aggression and seeks to bring out something different—an environment for growth, acceptance and peace (v. 7). It means listening with attentiveness to alternative views and opinions, accepting difference and diversity in humanity, in creation, and in people's relationships with God. Gentleness does not seek to control. It welcomes the chance to enter into discussion and put forward ideas, in a way that enables all to be heard and ensures that no one is 'put down'. True gentleness, as a character trait, should be seen as a strength, not a weakness. It will always seek to enable, to sustain, to support, and to bring out the best in another person (v. 12).

To know gentleness within our lives, do we first need to have discovered an inner peace, or does inner peace grow from gentleness in the way we live our own lives? The two qualities seem to sit alongside each other within the bowl holding the fruit of the Spirit.

For that reason, as well as showing gentleness with others, we should be gentle with ourselves. In Matthew 11:28–30, Jesus warns us that we are to beware of pushing our minds and bodies to the limit, into 'burn-out'. Instead, we are to find peace in his own gentleness of heart. If we do push ourselves too far, gentleness may be enforced upon us: we may be compelled to allow time for the body to rest, heal and recover. It may be that, at times, we need to find strength to hold painful memories and experiences that occasionally resurface, not being hard on ourselves, but seeking as much love and peace as possible, from others and from God.

4 Self-control

James 3:1–5, 13–18

In this passage we meet with James as he seeks to bring his readers some wisdom from above. As good works reveal faith, so, he believes, does wisdom, which is to be expressed in life through many gifts 'from above' (v. 17). James echoes the sentiments behind the Beatitudes (see Matthew 5:3–9) and the words of Jesus that true and false followers will be known by their fruits, either good or bad (7:16). The wisdom he teaches could be summarised as the discipline of self-control, which Paul includes among the fruit of the Spirit.

To have self-control in our lives, we need to know ourselves, to understand how we may react in certain circumstances—for example, recognising the limits of what we can cope with before we head off into anger, fear or despair. To exercise self-control is also to know and accept what we can change and what we can't, to know what we can do and what we can't. It means allowing and enabling others instead of always putting the self first.

In our personal lives, then, self-control may mean holding our tongue and thinking carefully before we speak (v. 2). It may also mean having a greater awareness of how much we eat and drink, how much we spend and how much (or how little) exercise we do. Exercising self-control may take us to concerns for the environment, perhaps thinking about the water we waste and how much we recycle. Only when we start to recycle do we realise how much waste clutters up our bins and our lives.

Spiritually, self-control calls us to remain focused upon God, to be diligent in prayer and committed to any work we offer to do. It means taking care of our spiritual and physical well-being, ensuring times of rest so that we keep God central on our Christian journey.

In what ways might you need to develop greater self-control, in speech, action or spiritual disciplines?

5 Love (III)

John 15:1–17

Today's title, 'Love (III)', is also the title of the famous poem 'Love bade me welcome', by the priest and poet George Herbert. In the poem, the person who speaks with God finds it difficult to accept the welcome and love that are offered by God. Instead, the speaker's focus is upon the possible reasons why he or she cannot come any closer to God. However, there is gentleness and determination within the depth of the love from which God speaks. There are words of forgiveness, hope and acceptance. Ultimately, the words spoken by God break down all the barriers that have been raised, before the invitation to come and eat is finally accepted.

Herbert's poem and the words in today's reading tell us that, in love, we are chosen by God and called by God to enter into the love that flows from the divine Trinity. We are called by love, just as we are, 'warts and all', for that is the person God has called. As Paul puts it, 'not many of you were wise… not many were powerful, not many were of noble birth. But God chose…' (1 Corinthians 1:26–27). In love, we are to bear the fruit of the Spirit that is already planted within us. We are to seek ways of allowing the fruit to mature and thrive, to have some pruned if necessary

(John 15:2), so that the work of God and the work of the Spirit appointed to us may not be lost.

The poem and the reading reveal the God who seeks our wholeness and well-being. True love builds us up; it is life-enhancing and life enriching, even though it may challenge and confront us along the way.

For the fruit of love to flourish, then, we need to pay loving attention to ourselves, to deepen the love we have for ourselves, for others and for God. To love is to remember the necessity to say sorry, to seek forgiveness, to be open to the needs of others and to our own needs. To enable love to bear lasting fruit, we need to spend time in quiet prayer with God, 'abiding' in him' (vv. 4–7), to discern and know that love of God personally and so to hear God 'bid us welcome'.

Herbert's poem is printed below. Read through it slowly, reflecting upon the words and on God's love. Love and forgiveness come together: what does it mean to you to receive the forgiveness of God and to know that God has called you just as you are?

> Love bade me welcome; yet my soul drew back,
> Guilty of dust and sin.
> But quick-eyed Love, observing me grow slack
> From my first entrance in,
> Drew nearer to me, sweetly questioning
> If I lacked anything.
>
> 'A guest,' I answered, 'worthy to be here.'
> Love said, 'You shall be he.'
> 'I, the unkind, ungrateful? Ah, my dear,
> I cannot look on thee.'
> Love took my hand, and smiling did reply,
> 'Who made the eyes but I?'
>
> 'Truth, Lord, but I have marred them; let my shame
> Go where it doth deserve.'
> 'And know you not,' says Love, 'who bore the blame?'
> 'My dear, then I will serve.'
> 'You must sit down,' says Love, 'and taste my meat.'
> So I did sit and eat.

6 The fruit of the Spirit

Galatians 5:16–26

Today's passage from Galatians draws all of the fruit of the Spirit together. We have a bowl filled with a wonderful selection of fruit. This Spirit-filled fruit bowl is very different from a literal fruit bowl, in which we place only the fruits that we like, leaving behind the ones we don't like on the shelf in the shop. As we have discovered, we cannot pick and choose which of the fruit of the Spirit to take and which to leave to one side: we are to embrace them all within the context of our daily lives.

The fruit of the Spirit may be familiar to us, but perhaps we do not so often consider the 'works of the flesh' that Paul lists in the preceding verses, to which the fruit of the Spirit is a 'contrast' (v. 22). In effect, we have two bowls to choose from, either of which will be influential in the way we live out our lives. There is one filled with the 'works of the flesh' (vv. 19–21), and the other filled with the 'fruit of the Spirit' (vv. 22–23).

Fruit left in a bowl for too long without being eaten will go 'off'. If we forget to nurture within us the Spirit-given fruit of faith, the temptation to turn to those of the 'flesh' will be much more difficult to fight against. The fruit will deteriorate through lack of care and use.

Allowing the fruit of the Spirit to give shape to our Christian faith and life, then, will help us not to become conceited, competitive or envious (v. 26). We are, of course, human, so there will be times when the temptations of the 'works of the flesh' take over. If the fruit of the Spirit is growing and maturing within us, though, we will find the strength to return to our true path in life and not be sidetracked for too long. This will mean returning to the God who, out of love, has chosen to plant within us the gift of life.

When you are tempted away from the 'fruit of the Spirit', how do you turn back to God? What do the 'works of the flesh' and the 'fruit of the Spirit' mean to you in your Christian journey?

Guidelines

At the end of these two weeks, what are your thoughts and feelings on the 'fruit' that we have been considering?

If you have plants, vegetables or fruit trees in your garden, you will know that they need the right soil and nourishment to ensure that they produce the 'fruit' that each one is meant to give. In the same way, if we are to bear the fruit of the Spirit, we need our lives to be rooted in God and nourished by prayer and the community of the church.

Faith draws from us many other good fruits that could also have been mentioned, which may be found intermingled with those that Paul wrote about to the Galatians. What other fruit of the Spirit would you include in the list, that you have been thinking about over the past two weeks?

FURTHER READING

Julian of Norwich, *Revelations of Divine Love*, Penguin, 1966

Richard Rolle, *The Fire of Love*, Penguin, 1981

John of the Cross: Selected Writings (Classics of Western Spirituality), Paulist Press, 1987

Meet the Holy Spirit

Not so long ago, a series like this would have begun by describing the Holy Spirit as the forgotten person of the Trinity. We can't say that now. The rise of the charismatic movement in the West and the astonishing spread of Pentecostal Christianity across the global South have led many Christians to be intensely focused on (one aspect of) the work of the Spirit. That brings its own dangers, however: it is easy to forget the breadth of the biblical witness to the Spirit's work, or even to see the Spirit as a power rather than a person.

This week and next, we look at who the Spirit is and what the Spirit does. The Spirit appears right at the beginning of the Bible, 'hovering over the face' of the primal waters of creation (Genesis 1:2). Through the Old Testament, we find references to 'the Spirit of God' alongside references to 'the angel of the Lord' and 'the word of the Lord'. At times, these divine agents seem to be identified directly with God (Judges 13:21–22; Exodus 3:2, 6). In the New Testament, this hint that the one God's life is somehow plural settles into a conviction that God the Father works in the world through God's Son (who, though always existing, becomes human in Jesus of Nazareth) and God's Spirit, who is sent in a new and permanent way on the church at Pentecost. We need to note, then, that the Holy Spirit is truly and fully God, no less so than the Father and the Son. As we will see, according to the Bible, the Spirit is involved in the work of creation, makes believers holy, reveals God's truth and performs other works that only God can perform.

In our second week of readings, we will look at our experience of the Spirit in prayer, worship, teaching and holiness—including the area of spiritual gifts. The argument among Christians over spiritual gifts is not about whether they exist, or what they are, but whether some (but only some) were temporary. Depending on how we count, there are about 35 different spiritual gifts mentioned in the New Testament. Many of them are completely uncontroversial: to speak of someone as 'a gifted preacher' or 'having a real gift for evangelism' is normal in every strand of the church. Others are largely forgotten, but equally unexceptional when recalled: Paul speaks of administration as a spiritual gift (1 Corinthians 12:28). Some, however, involve miraculous abilities, largely healing or special forms of revelation (tongues; words of knowledge; prophecy), and there is disagreement over whether these were temporary gifts, given to enable the church to become established, but now withdrawn, or whether we should look for such works of the Spirit still.

This is a relatively minor disagreement: Christians can and do agree on almost everything about who the Holy Spirit is and what he does. The disagreement can be very visible and, tragically, has caused pain and division; it is not a major split in belief, however, and most of what the Spirit does in the life of the church is uncontroversial, and shared by all strands of Christian belief.

Unless otherwise stated, quotations are taken from the New Revised Standard Version of the Bible.

1 Father, Son, and Spirit

Matthew 3:11—4:2

A baptism is a big deal, of course, and, when Jesus is baptised, the whole family turns up! Our reading begins with John's prophecy about Jesus. 'Baptise' literally means 'plunge under' or 'immerse' (it is what you do to a piece of cloth to dye it in classical Greek), although it acquired an important ritual meaning in Judaism, describing a purifying bathing, particularly of Gentile converts to Judaism. John's talk of baptism 'with the Holy Spirit and fire' recalls a Jewish belief that a flood of fire would cover the world and cleanse it of sin (see also Isaiah 4:4, which speaks of a cleansing 'spirit of burning'). Jesus, in John's prophecy, comes to bring this cleansing, as well as a final separating judgment (3:12).

When Jesus comes to John, John initially refuses to baptise him: baptism is an act of repentance, and John sees that Jesus has nothing to repent of. Indeed, the roles should be reversed, and he should be baptised by Jesus. John does not understand that Jesus' whole reason for coming is to identify with broken and sinful people, himself to bear their guilt and shame, and so to bring salvation.

When Jesus is baptised, the Father's voice is heard, affirming his mission, and the Spirit descends on Jesus in the form of a dove. The Spirit here appears as the one who is the bond of love between the Father and the Son, coming from the Father to the Son in a sign of affirmation and love.

All of the Gospels speak of Jesus being anointed by the Spirit at the beginning of his ministry. From the point of his baptism on, Jesus is led and guided by the Spirit. In Matthew 4:1, that leading takes a strange turn: the Spirit leads Jesus into the desert, to fast and to suffer temptation. For Jesus to fulfil his calling, he has to face and overcome all the temptations that are the common lot of humanity, and so the Spirit leads him straight into that battle. We too have to accept that the Spirit's leading will take us to the right places, the necessary places, rather than the easy or desirable places.

2 The Spirit and Jesus

Isaiah 61:1–11

In this passage, the prophet speaks in the voice of one who will come, who will bring God's promised future to the people of Israel. These chapters of Isaiah are addressed to the people who have returned from exile in Babylon, who have experienced the joy and hope of the end of exile but now face the hard reality of building a new life in the ruins of the once-great city, Jerusalem. The words of the prophecy invite them to look forward to a further, and this time decisive, act of divine deliverance: the God who brought them back from exile will one day exalt them among the nations. This promise echoes through the last eleven chapters of Isaiah: in chapter 61 it is the vision of the central verses, 4–7.

As the middle chapters of Isaiah spoke repeatedly of a coming Servant who would establish God's rule, so here we have one anointed with the Spirit to bring God's purposes to fruition. Of course, in Luke's account, Jesus began his ministry by deliberately taking these verses and claiming that he was the fulfilment of them. In Luke 4, Jesus stops his reading halfway through verse 2 of the Isaiah text as we have it. He proclaims the 'year of the Lord's favour' but does not mention 'the day of vengeance of our God', perhaps because his first coming was to bring salvation: judgment would wait longer.

The anointing of the Spirit here is empowerment for a mission. The mission is to bring salvation, but God's salvation is described in wide-ranging terms. 'Bringing good news to the poor' speaks of economic transformation: those who had returned from exile were scratching out a living on a heap of ruins, so this promise must have been powerful and direct for them. 'Binding up the broken-hearted' takes us to spiritual and emotional transformation, which is what we usually think of when we talk about salvation. 'Liberty to the captives and release to the prisoners' speaks of political transformation.

The original hearers would have interpreted all this in terms of the restoration of the fortunes of David's kingdom. As we have seen, though, Jesus had something else in mind, something much bigger—a different kingdom that would transform the whole world.

3 The Spirit and creation

Psalm 104:24–35

We tend to think of the Holy Spirit at work in the church, but the biblical witness goes much wider than that. We noted in the Introduction that the Spirit was present at the beginning of the work of creation; in this psalm we see the Spirit's continuing work in the created order, giving life to God's creatures.

The psalm is a simple song of worship to God, which focuses on God's power and majesty displayed in creation. (Robert Grant's famous hymn 'O worship the king' is based in part on this psalm.) The early verses speak of the grandeur of the mountains, rivers and seas; verses 14–17 move to the life of plants, and the second half of the psalm focuses on animals. Through it all, there is a stress on God's wisdom in arranging the disparate parts of creation to work together: springs and streams quench the thirst of animals, while trees, forests and mountains provide homes for them. The verses we are reading begin with a note of praise in verse 24, before thinking about the inhabitants of the seas. Leviathan (v. 26) was a name for a sea-monster common in the myths of the ancient Near Eastern peoples; the psalmist insists that even such a mythical personification of evil is, in fact, God's creature, 'formed to frolic' (NIV)!

God has a close and ongoing relationship to the creation, according to verses 27–30. He gives creatures their food, and his graciousness or absence is central to their flourishing. The psalmist plays on the ambiguity in the Hebrew word *ruach*, which can mean wind or breath or Spirit, in verses 29–30. Animals need breath to live, and their breath is identified poetically with God's Spirit, who brings renewal to all the earth.

The Holy Spirit is present and active in all of creation, bringing life and renewal. When Paul preaches in Athens and tells his hearers that God 'is not far from any one·of us', quoting a poet who said, 'In him we live and move and have our being' (Acts 17:27–28), it is the particular work of God the Holy Spirit that is in view—God present and active in the world, bringing the gift of life. As the psalmist was, we should be ready not only to see a testimony to God's great power in creation but also to know that God is constantly and intimately involved in the world he has made.

4 The Spirit who helps

John 14:15–31

In chapters 14—17 of his Gospel, John invites us to overhear Jesus' last extended period of teaching to his disciples, in the upper room, before he is arrested in Gethsemane later that night. Jesus knows what is coming—his arrest and death; then, too, his resurrection and ascension—and spends his time trying to help his followers understand the reasons for his 'going away'. He asks the disciples to accept, out of love for him, that this is God's plan and so for the best (vv. 28–31). He also says that it will be better for the disciples if he goes, in part because, when he goes, he will send the Spirit, who will never leave (vv. 16–17).

Jesus' 'going away' in these texts is complicated: he is speaking both of his impending death and of his coming ascension, which will follow the resurrection. We, of course, can see this; the disciples could not, so when Jesus speaks of 'going away' he is referring sometimes to his death (for example, in 16:16) and sometimes to his ascension (for example, 14:19).

Jesus speaks of the Holy Spirit as 'another Advocate/Comforter/Helper' (vv. 16, 26) and as the 'Spirit of truth' (v. 17). The word used in verse 16 is 'paraclete', a Greek word that originally referred to a friend who argued your case in court but came to have a wide range of meanings, all of them suggesting someone who offered support or spoke on your behalf. Jesus promises that the Spirit will come as a supportive friend who will teach believers truth and remind them of everything that he has taught (v. 26). The Spirit will be with us permanently (v. 16), not leaving after a time, as Jesus had to. Jesus also promises that the Spirit will be 'in' or 'among' believers (v. 17). The phrase is ambiguous: it could mean 'present in each believer' and it could mean 'present in the community of believers'. We know from elsewhere in scripture that the Spirit does fill both individual believers and the church; so perhaps the ambiguity is deliberate, with both meanings intended.

5 The Spirit of power

Acts 1:1–11

Acts begins with a brief account of the 40 days that Jesus spent teaching his followers after rising from the dead, before he ascended into heaven. The main theme of his teaching was 'the kingdom of God' (v. 3), but the text focuses on his teaching about the coming Holy Spirit. The disciples are to wait for 'the promise of the Father', the promise being that they will be 'baptised in the Holy Spirit' (vv. 4–5).

When they come together for the last time, immediately before Jesus' ascension to be with the Father, the disciples ask about the restoration of David's empire (v. 6), but Jesus' reply again focuses on the coming Spirit: 'You will receive power when the Spirit comes' (v. 8).

This language of 'power' might make some readers feel uncomfortable, particularly so close to the phrase 'baptism in the Spirit', which has been adopted within certain Christian circles in recent years to describe a particular experience of empowering by the Spirit, usually accompanied by apparently supernatural gifts. As we have seen, 'baptism' means immersion, and Jesus seems to be describing the coming experience of the fulfilment of Father God's promise by comparing it to the baptism in water, which had been a part of the disciples' experience.

'Power' here is clearly to be understood as power to witness effectively to Jesus, from Jerusalem to the ends of the world (v. 8). (Indeed, it was understood like this in early Pentecostalism, with baptism in the Spirit being seen as an anointing for mission.) In Acts, witness includes miraculous healings and exorcisms (ch. 3—4; 16:16–18), but the emphasis is not on the miracles themselves so much as on the demonstration they give that God has come decisively in Jesus.

In verse 2 we read that Jesus' own teaching was given in the power of the Spirit. Most interesting, perhaps, is the little word 'began' in verse 1. Luke's Gospel is about what Jesus 'began to do and to teach'; Acts will be about the continuation of Jesus' ministry. The church in the power of the Spirit continues the work of Jesus, witnessing in actions and in words to what God has done in sending Jesus.

6 The Spirit of wisdom

1 Corinthians 2

The Corinthian Christians thought they knew all about the Holy Spirit. When it came to supernatural gifts, particularly the gift of tongues, they excelled—and they were proud of it. Paul's response was not to condemn the gifts, which were valuable in their place (ch. 12—14), but to give a much bigger, fuller picture of who the Holy Spirit is and what he does.

In the passage we are reading, Paul is taking aim at the idea that the Spirit's wisdom is shown through eloquence and impressive speech (vv. 1–4). Looking and sounding impressive in worldly terms is not good evidence of God at work—a fact that Paul links to the heart of the gospel story, the crucifixion of Jesus. The cross of Christ is foolishness to Greeks (1:23), yet it is the place where God's wisdom is found. The Spirit 'searches everything', even God's purposes (2:10). The truly spiritual, then, do know wisdom, but it is a different wisdom—God's wisdom, not worldly wisdom (v. 6). Enlightened by the Spirit, we are enabled to understand God's ways and God's purposes.

Paul draws a strong contrast here between the wisdom of the world and divine wisdom. No doubt, the strength of the contrast is explained partly by the needs of his argument with the Corinthian church, but we have to take it seriously, even allowing for this context. The crucifixion appeared to be an ignominious defeat and humiliation for Jesus, yet it was the decisive moment in God's victory, and this sets the pattern for all

God's ways. If we see the world with the wisdom of the Holy Spirit, we will see that apparently trivial things are, in fact, important, and many of the 'big issues' that are endlessly rehearsed in our media and conversations are really of little moment. We will also judge events with a different system of values. The passage challenges us to catch hold of the Spirit's wisdom and so to think differently about, potentially, everything.

Guidelines

The Holy Spirit gives support and help, power and wisdom to believers. There is much comfort in these promises, and we should not ignore it. Jesus' great promises about the coming of the Spirit in John 14 are all about offering comfort to the disciples in the face of coming tragedy.

Every Christian can remember times when, in the face of trouble or danger, God's presence seemed especially close. A warm and joyous sense of peace or love can surround us and support us, and that is a real gift from God. We can and should pray for others who need to know God's help, and, indeed, give thanks for those times we can look back on— sometimes only later realising just how much we were sustained by God.

That said, the work of the Holy Spirit in scripture is much bigger than just offering comfort to believers. We have seen that the Bible speaks of the Spirit at work in the whole world, bringing life and breath to every living creature. We have also seen that the work of the Spirit in the church and the life of the believer is repeatedly about mission. The work of the Spirit is the spreading of the knowledge of God's mercy and love across the whole world, until God's justice and joy are known everywhere. There is an end worth praying for!

26 August–1 September

1 The fruit of the Spirit

Galatians 5:13–26

Paul has spent much of Galatians insisting that Christians are free from the Jewish law; here, at the end, he turns to warn them against drawing the wrong conclusions. The point is not that 'anything goes' but that freedom from the law is a call to a higher vision of holiness. 'Do not use your freedom as an opportunity for self-indulgence,' he warns (v. 13); instead, we should fulfil an open-ended commitment to love, and so live a more perfect life.

As often in Paul's letters, he describes the new life we are to live as 'living by the Spirit' (v. 16). Here, this is contrasted with 'the works of the flesh' (v. 19) or 'gratifying the desires of the flesh' (v. 16). Some translations have 'sinful nature' for 'flesh', which perhaps helps us not to misunderstand Paul's point. He is not denouncing our physicality or embodiedness (we who believe that God became incarnate can never regard the body as evil) but is using 'flesh' as shorthand for our broken and misshapen hearts, which desire wrongly. The 'works of the flesh' he lists range widely but there is some focus on failures to love: 'enmities, strife, jealousy, anger, quarrels, dissensions, factions' (v. 20).

Paul then offers another list—the well-known 'fruit of the Spirit' (vv. 22–23). It is striking that the list in verses 19–21 is of 'works' and this one is of 'fruit'. Paul seems to be suggesting a contrast between things we do and things that naturally grow in us. It is also noticeable that 'fruit' is singular: what grows is a new character, marked by all these various virtues.

Just as freedom is not an invitation to licentiousness, so this language of fruit is not an invitation to inaction. Paul calls us to 'live by the Spirit' (v. 16) and to 'be guided by the Spirit' (v. 25). Every day there are choices to be made, to refuse some actions and adopt other attitudes. As days turn into years, the effect of the accumulation of such choices will be a way of life, marked by varying degrees of self-indulgence and virtue. Paul invites us to make every choice well, and so to grow in the life of the Spirit.

2 The Spirit of mission

Acts 4:1–31

These are the very early days of the church in Jerusalem. In Acts 3, Peter and John have just healed a man from a congenital disability and have used the resulting amazement to testify to Jesus' resurrection. We pick up the story as the alarmed authorities arrest and question them. The apostles are threatened and warned to stop speaking about Jesus, and are released. The response of the young church is to pray.

The Holy Spirit is mentioned three times in this passage, in verses 8, 25 and 31. Each time, the work of the Spirit is to enable someone—Peter, a psalmist (here identified as David) and all the believers—to speak well about Jesus. Peter is given courage and eloquence in order to speak powerfully in a terrifying context, in the face of a hostile crowd of the nation's rulers. The believers together are enabled to 'speak the word of God with boldness'. The psalmist is slightly different, of course. He is enabled to prophesy truthfully, to write inspired scripture, but the message is still the same—Jesus, his gospel and his mission.

Alongside the call to holiness, the other major New Testament theme of the work of the Spirit in the believer's life, and in the corporate life of the church, is mission. The Spirit witnesses to the truth of the gospel of Jesus (1 John 5:6); the Spirit grants courage, boldness, wisdom and eloquence to those who are called to testify to Jesus in the hard and dangerous places; the Spirit enables us to understand the scripture that he himself has inspired and to read the 'signs of the times' so that we can find convincing and relevant ways of speaking the truth, as Peter does here (vv. 8–12).

Although the three direct references to the work of the Spirit here have to do with speaking, in the believers' prayer we see that works of mercy, and miracles, are just as much part of their vision of mission (v. 30). To point towards Jesus in word and deed: this is the heart of our Christian vocation and at the heart of what the Holy Spirit wants to grow in our lives.

3 The gifts of the Spirit

1 Corinthians 12:1–30

This famous passage has become the go-to text for discussion of supernatural gifts in the church today. We should note, however, that Paul's main point is not to list or encourage supernatural gifts but to provide a context for the use of all gifts—from teaching to working miracles (v. 28). Here we learn more about how the gifts of the Spirit should be used in the church than about what different gifts the Spirit gives.

Paul begins with a quick rehearsal of a crucial point: the Spirit's concern is to enable believers to witness to Jesus. The primary test of any supposed manifestation of the Holy Spirit, then, is whether Jesus is exalted or denigrated. Paul puts this in stark terms (v. 3), but the point is more general: if at any time we think we are being led by the Spirit but the name of Jesus is being dishonoured, we can be sure that we are wrong.

After saying this, Paul moves to his major point, which is the need for unity in the church, particularly in the context of a diversity of gifting. Diversity is real but all the richness of the diversity comes from the one source, the Holy Spirit (vv. 4–11), and for one purpose, the building up of the church ('the common good', v. 7). Paul develops this theme with his illustration of the church as a body, made up of many different parts, each with different functions. Diversity is necessary so that the body can do what it is designed to do (vv. 14–20).

This gets more delicate as the question of differing status is brought up (vv. 21–25). Some gifts, some roles in the church, are more valued than others. Paul does not say that this is wrong (indeed, we are to desire 'the greater gifts' eagerly: v. 31); instead, he suggests that within the body we actively compensate for such disparities by treating those lacking honour in an especially honouring way.

We could and should apply this teaching in many church contexts, but consider just one: if our debates over charismatic gifting had taken the teaching of 1 Corinthians 12 seriously—if we had been serious about intentionally honouring those who seem to have the least status—how differently might some of the arguments have gone?

4 The Spirit of prayer

Romans 8:12–27

In Romans 8, Paul gives us several glimpses of the work of the Spirit in the life of the believer. First, the Spirit leads us (v. 14). In the context, the meaning is clearly ethical: the Spirit shows us how to live a true Christian life, holy and righteous (see v. 13). Paul then speaks of 'the Spirit of adoption' (v. 15), suggesting that the gift of the indwelling Spirit is intimately linked to our adoption into God's family. In graphic language, Paul suggests that the Spirit cries out this truth in our hearts: 'Abba! Father!'

Paul's gaze turns next to the future, when the salvation promised by God, already experienced in the gift of the Spirit and in the reality of our adoption, will come to full flower. Creation itself—the whole cosmos—is waiting eagerly, groaning in desire for salvation to come. And believers, those who are given the Spirit, groan along with creation (v. 23). As we wait, the Spirit is at work within us, praying, interceding with 'sighs too deep for words' (v. 26) when we do not know how to pray.

Verse 26 has sometimes been taken as a description of 'praying in tongues'. This is not wrong, I believe: the experience of people who pray in tongues can often sound very much like this, being led to pray in ways they do not understand. However, I think that the promise here is wider and deeper than just the gift of tongues. God's Spirit opens our hearts to the pain and the needs of the world, gives us wisdom to see the things that really matter, and leads us to pray well for those needs.

The language describing the Spirit's work within us here is powerful: the Spirit cries, groans and sighs, expressing exuberant faith in God's salvation and an urgent desire to see it come in fullness. The Spirit inspires prayer in the hearts of believers—prayer based on utter confidence in God; prayer expressing anguish at the present broken state of the world. Praying like this is, in God's good purposes, a part we can play in bringing to pass the final healing of everything that we, and the whole cosmos, long for. Let us pray!

5 The Spirit builds the church

Ezekiel 37:1–14

This is another famous text, and another image of bodies and their different parts. It is another example, too, of the ambiguous Hebrew word *ruach*, which can mean 'Spirit', 'wind' or 'breath'. Ezekiel prophesied during the exile, when it seemed that all of the hopes of God's people were dashed. This powerful vision speaks directly into that felt despair:

a valley full of dry bones, representing the death of Israel's hope and life (v. 11), is miraculously given new life, offering a promise of hope to the broken people (v. 14).

The prophet sees and examines the bones (v. 2). The question comes: is there hope? 'Can these bones live?' (v. 3). Ezekiel is marked by his humility before God, and here he refuses either faithless despair or presumption about what God will do: 'Lord, you alone know.' Then comes the first of two calls to prophesy. In response to Ezekiel's first prophecy, directed at the bones (v. 4), the bones come together into complete skeletons, linked by tendons; they are clothed with flesh and covered in skin. It is a miracle of recreation—but they are still so many corpses. God calls Ezekiel to prophesy to the Spirit/wind/breath (v. 9); as he does, the corpses come to life and become a great army.

This prophecy is about Israel's return from exile, but it presents a wider vision of the Holy Spirit bringing new life to God's people whenever and wherever they are dry and broken. The twofold nature of the prophecy and the miracle is striking: God's word addressed directly to us can and will recreate us, but only the coming of the Spirit can fill us with new life. The emphasis of the text is on God's word being spoken, proclaimed faithfully in response to God's command. At the decisive point, though, the proclaimed word is the occasion for the Spirit's coming and bringing the longed-for new life.

We must not be too quick to read our own situations into this passage. Exile was the failure of all God's promises because of the sin of the people, so it was something drastic and historic; our sense that the worship in our church is a little flat is not what the passage is about! There is a general pattern to learn from, however: as the Spirit gives life and breath to God's creatures, so the Spirit gives life to God's people.

6 The Spirit poured out

Acts 2:1–21

Ten days after Jesus had ascended into heaven after his resurrection, the promised Holy Spirit came upon the believers. Luke focuses at some length on the other languages that they are enabled to speak (vv. 4–12), including a list of the nations whose inhabitants heard their own languages. The description recalls the tower of Babel story, in which a primordial single human language was confused and split (Genesis 11:1–9); here, human language is not reunited but the divisions imposed by linguistic differences are miraculously overcome. Genesis 11, coming just before the account of Abram and Sarai's ancestry and call, is the last chapter of the prehistorical account of the failure and disintegration of human community that fills the early chapters of our Bible. At Pentecost, there is a visible sign (in the new community that Jesus has founded, the church, and through the Holy Spirit coming on the church) that such ancient curses and divisions are finally, by God's grace, being healed.

At the time, of course, no one understood this. Most were confused; some mocked (vv. 12–13). So Peter attempts to explain what is happening, referring to a prophecy from the book of Joel. The prophecy emphasises that this event is at the beginning of God's final re-creation of all things ('in the last days...' v. 17), which will end with a cosmic cataclysm and the return of Jesus, bringing salvation to all God's people (vv. 19–21). In between, the great stress is on the fact that God's gift of the Spirit is universal. Divisions of age, gender and social status are all transcended by this divine gift, which comes to sons and daughters, young and old, male and female servants. All, without distinction or exception, will receive the promised Spirit.

The church is to be the living sign of the new community that God is bringing into being in Jesus. This is a community where the barriers that divide human beings—age, gender, ethnicity, nationality—are broken down and forgotten. What would it look like to live out this reality, this gift of the Spirit, in your community today? Could your church do those things?

Guidelines

Prayer, fruit, gifts—and a vision of a new community of justice and joy that breaks down every barrier dividing human beings from each other; there has been a lot to get excited about in this week's readings. The work of the Spirit is to form a new community of renewed people, changed and equipped to spread the reality of the kingdom to every corner of the earth.

Prayer is at the heart of this. Prayer changes situations and changes us—or, better, God changes situations, and changes us, through our prayers. Living closely with God, we grow the fruit of the Spirit in our lives and receive the gifts of the Spirit to be more effective in the Spirit's work. The gifts are given to build the church, the community of the Spirit, that exists to do the work of mission, of bringing the good news of the kingdom to all.

Each of us can pause and ask, what is my part in this great move of the Holy Spirit? How am I growing and being gifted? How can I be a part of the kingdom purposes of God? 'Every corner of the earth', after all, includes the street I live on, the place I work in and the shops and homes I visit, not just far-off lands.

The BRF
Magazine

The Managing Editor writes...

Spirituality, discipleship and mission—we sometimes talk about these elements of Christian life as if they're separate from each other, almost in different 'boxes'. Perhaps we think of spirituality as for the more contemplative among us, discipleship for the practical servant types and mission for the self-confident extraverts. Yet all three are interrelated and are all important parts of BRF's overall vision.

In her report on 'International Messy Church', Lucy Moore expresses a sense of great excitement as Messy Church continues to spread worldwide, with ever-expanding networks of people involved in this mission to families outside 'traditional' church. Our 'Recommended reading' in this issue also offers books that focus on the more outward-looking elements—evangelism in today's culture, discipleship in Messy Church and active service in the church and the world.

In the third of these books, *Servant Ministry*, Tony Horsfall writes, 'The reflective life... is valid only if it is expressed outwardly in tangible acts of service, and love for God is real only when it leads to love for others.' But of course (as I'm sure Tony would agree), when we love and serve others, and when we engage with people outside the church, we become more and more aware of the needs in the world around us, which sends us back to reflection and prayer—and so the cycle goes on.

Sally Smith's article on our revamped creative prayer and spirituality journal, *Quiet Spaces*, describes a new direction for the journal, which we hope will stimulate readers (as Sally says) 'to grow in their relationship with God and to keep prayer as a central part of their lives'. Finally, our chosen book extract, from *Spiritual Care of Dying and Bereaved People*, focuses on the spiritual identity at the the core of every individual.

Whatever we consider to be our own major gifts and calling in the Christian life, spirituality, discipleship and mission are all equally vital, each interwoven with and constantly feeding into one another. We hope that BRF can continue to inspire you to develop all three strands in your own walk with God.

Lisa Cherrett

International Messy Church

Lucy Moore

'All the ends of the earth will remember and turn to the Lord, and all the families of the nations will bow down before him' (Psalm 22:27, NIV). When he mentions 'bowing', I don't think the psalmist had in mind painting, constructing, exploding, glueing, jumping, inventing, dancing, running, shouting, laughing and eating before the Lord, but perhaps he would have been happy to know that so many families from so many nations across the world take such delight in their Lord and Creator, albeit expressing it in different ways.

We've been thrilled and intrigued to see Messy Church spreading to different countries and continents over the last eight years, and to hear stories of families all over the world coming back to church, or coming to church for the first time, and enjoying it enough to keep coming.

Back in the ancient history of seven years ago, when Messy Church was just a handful of local churches giving it a try, Fresh Expressions came across the idea and asked if they could film it for their first DVD promoting the idea of fresh expressions of church. The DVD was duly despatched to Fresh Expressions associates, who used it in their training across the world. Very early in the development of Messy Church, therefore, we were receiving emails from countries as far flung as New Zealand and Canada, asking how they could get going with a Messy Church of their own. 'We saw it in the DVD and it looks really good…'

There is also a certain amount of gossip! People from our own church came back from a cruise describing how they had befriended an Australian couple, had found out they were all Christians and had started sharing stories of what their different churches do, including Messy Church. 'And they were so interested! They want to start one in Adelaide! Now I must send them a book about it!'

We currently have several international speakers who are enthusiastic to include Messy Church as a tool for churches to use. Our dear Danish friend, Bjarne Gertz Olsen, speaks at many events in Eastern Europe and emailed today saying, 'Soon I shall go to Slovakia to

European Lutheran Sunday School Associations conference. Here will be participants from… Germany, Georgia, Belarus, Ukraine, Poland, Slovakia, Estonia, Latvia, Romania, Denmark. I will like here to make an exhibition about Messy Church and also inform about Messy Church.'

As you can imagine, the impact of sharing the idea across all those countries could be huge. Another friend, Marty Woods from Fusion, has been speaking around the world at different training events and emailed, 'We have just come back from a Sports Conference in Orlando… Great time: 127 countries with over 540 people… Many are interested in Messy Church—particularly in the Ukraine. They have 15,000 churches that they are contacting and working with in some way, preparing for the Euro Cup. They respond most to the idea of the Sunday after the Opening Ceremony having a Messy Church…' and later: 'Been on the move, flying back from Poland, and they are really keen about Messy Church there. Plan to run them after our festivals at the Euro Cup in at least three places I am aware of.'

So where do we know of Messy Churches happening outside the UK? The countries we *know* of are Canada, New Zealand, Australia, the USA, Denmark, Germany, Poland, South Africa, Switzerland, Norway, Grenada, Spain, Ireland and the Falklands. Some of these have just one isolated Messy Church: Spain's was set up in the English Chaplaincy on the Costa del Sol after I spoke at the Synod in Portugal. South Africa's is run by someone who came across the idea while visiting relatives in the UK. Poland's was started by a Salvation Army officer who had been introduced to the idea through her Army networks. Switzerland's is, again, a set of family relationships sharing a good thing around. The way Kreativ Kirke began in Norway remains a mystery!

Sue Kalbfleisch and Nancy Rowe are doing a fantastic job in Eastern Canada, leading training and keeping Messy Churches in touch with each other, and there are at least 20 happening there. One vicar has written her academic research on it. There isn't much encouragement from the church authorities there yet, but we hope and trust that there will be when they understand more about it.

In New Zealand, Julie Hintz is building a network and series of training events for their growing numbers of Messy Churches. They prefer to be reasonably independent of 'colonial' ideas so we are encouraging a sense of interdependence and working with Julie to create good links.

Australia feels full of Messy friends since our trips in 2011 and 2012, and Sydney-based Judyth Roberts is responding to requests for help there as part of her job within the Uniting Church.

In the States, we are looking forward to things taking off after my trip to the USA in November, which may focus the energy building up there through isolated Messy Churches and through the efforts of Andrew Holmes, Our Man in Indianapolis.

Denmark is an interesting case as they have worked from top down rather than grassroots up like the rest of us. The Danish Sunday School Association became excited about the book and concept when talking to Richard and Karen at the Frankfurt Book Fair and decided to go for it wholeheartedly as an organisation, with their own website and resources in Danish. They currently have about 25 Messy Churches, backed by a Regional Coordinator, Karen Markusson.

Charis Lambert took Messy Church out to Zimbabwe with members of her team and the Zimkids charity. She writes of one of the events they led:

Our Messy Church in Mutoko started a day earlier than expected as 60 people turned up at the church, having walked 14km to see us. We could not disappoint their enthusiasm so we spent a couple of hours with them making bracelets, playing with playdough and introducing them to our parachute games, before giving them some sandwiches and sending them home. To our amazement they all returned the next morning for more! ...

Our training was simplified for this very mixed-age audience and needed to be translated into Shona by the local pastor and our Zimkids team... We sat everyone under the trees and realised that we had about 200 people sitting together. We demonstrated how to fold paper and make a cross with just one cut—to show how useful it is to do something in order to aid our understanding. We started some singing and were blown away by the exuberance of the Shona worship! After lunch, people kept on arriving, adding themselves to the already overcrowded parachutes, the games of soccer and the craft activities—more donkeys!

We finished the afternoon at about 5pm after serving tea to approximately 300 people—no mean feat in a church with no kitchen facilities and no electricity or running water!

At BRF we have the interesting job of trying to balancing the needs of the UK Messy network with the needs of the networks in other countries, trying to respond appropriately and effectively without killing off the team members with excessive travel demands. But most of all we have the privilege of getting excited by and with this wonderful movement of God's Spirit as he finds his way to reach families in so many different places and contexts.

Lucy Moore heads up BRF's Messy Church ministry. For more information, visit www.messychurch.org.uk.

New editor for *Quiet Spaces*

Sally Smith

Until recently I worked in education publishing, producing materials for teaching Christianity in RE lessons. My work there built on years spent in classrooms and gave me a new set of skills in editing and project management. But then I heard I was being made redundant. After the normal panic, I began to wonder what I could do. The whole process was steeped in prayer, with many people praying for and with me, and, in a strange way, I felt privileged to recognise God's involvement in the whole process. God didn't tell me what was next; he just promised that the future would contain gold and jewels.

I like to have everything planned out, so, although this was comforting, it was also, to my eyes, unsatisfactory: what would a 'gold' future look like? What would I be doing? What reason would I have to get up in the morning? How was God going to weave together the editing, spirituality and education strands that were all equally important to me? But God was true to his promise and provided more than I could have imagined.

I had long used and admired *Quiet Spaces* so being asked to take the best of *Quiet Spaces* and merge it with the concept of Bible reading notes seemed a dream request. I was being asked to produce the publication I had been looking for on bookshop shelves but had failed to find. At first it felt self-indulgent: imagine what you would like and then make it happen! But as I talked to other people about the idea, I was encouraged: they were asking when it would be out and how they could get a copy. They wanted to develop their prayer life and keep it fresh and creative. Bible reading notes provided a brilliant structure and were feeding these people intellectually, but they were looking for something else as well, for ways of engaging with God on a different level. They wanted to develop their walk with God in practical ways.

So the idea grew. Take a theme for two weeks and explore that theme in a range of different ways, allowing for different personalities and styles. Include some classic writers on prayer, some traditional approaches, and be creative and innovative as well.

It soon became apparent that the format needed to be flexible. It would be no good telling readers to explore a Bible passage artistically on a day when they barely had time to stop—if on another day they could devote a whole hour or so to a prayer walk. So the individual elements needed to be undated, with readers being encouraged to use the most appropriate element for them on any particular day. The message would be: if you miss a day or find something that doesn't appeal, that's OK, you can try something else. If you only get halfway through, you can come back and finish it tomorrow. Or you can do several elements in one day, creating a personal quiet day when you have time and space to try something new.

There began to be a rhythm to each theme, with some elements being longer or shorter, more or less involved, active, creative or thoughtful. The rhythm fitted across a day—from the morning, when concentration levels are often higher, through to the afternoon, when concentration is lower and something more active or practical is useful, and on into the evening, when we often become more reflective and want to look back on the day. The rhythm worked across a week as well, with some days when we have energy and time and are able to put more of ourselves into our prayer life, and other days when we just want to be fed.

With this flexibility came a sense of freedom. Readers could use the material as suited them best, but there was always the possibility of simply taking one element a day and working through the book in order. There are times when we need the comfort that such structures bring.

I have tried to include some of the classic writers on prayer, to explore how we can learn from them, as well as using the Bible in prayer and, of course, retaining the themes that *Quiet Spaces* has traditionally been so good at addressing. The writers have come up with some creative ways of entering the themes and responding to them, enabling readers to grow in their relationship with God and to keep prayer as a central part of their lives.

It has certainly been a period of gold and jewels for me, bringing together my editing skills and my experience of leading and attending quiet days and retreats. It has been an exciting adventure to produce the new *Quiet Spaces*. I have worked with some great writers who have caught the vision and produced excellent materials, which have already enhanced my prayer life, leading me on that journey to and with God.

Sally Smith is a spiritual director in Southwell and Nottingham diocese, where she also leads quiet days and is part of a deanery group exploring spirituality outside the church. She has a Diploma in Theological and Pastoral Studies.

Recommended reading

Our recommended reading for this issue focuses on the important question of church and how it can bring its mission strategy and tactics up to date, to address today's challenges. How can the issues of effectively engaging unchurched local communities be explained and taken forward? How does the church move people within its influence to a deeper commitment—beyond theoretical faith to real discipleship? What are the responsibilities of those who support leaders in their task of contemporary evangelism and discipleship? These are not new questions, but declining church attendance demands a revaluation of the current approach. BRF is pleased to offer this group of new titles to further the progress of the debate and help provide solutions to these vital issues.

The Word's Out
Speaking the gospel today
David Male and Paul Weston

At a time when few people attend church, evangelism is more important than ever. The problem is that churches and individuals often struggle with the idea because their approach is no longer culturally appropriate.

This book aims to reform, reimagine and renew a theology, vision and practice for evangelism. An invaluable resource for church leaders, its approach is theologically rigorous and powerfully practical, focusing on redefining a genuine biblical evangelism. What does it mean to be an 'evangelist' now? If it isn't our primary gifting, how can we facilitate it in our church? And how can we connect not just with those on the fringes but with those who are way outside?

The Revd David Male is Director of the Centre for Pioneer Learning and Tutor in Pioneer Mission Training at Ridley Hall and Westcott House, Cambridge, and Fresh Expressions Adviser for Ely Diocese. The Revd Dr Paul Weston is Tutor in Mission and Homiletics at Ridley Hall, Cambridge.

paperback, 978 0 85746 169 8, £8.99, 224 pages
Also available for Kindle: please visit www.brfonline.org.uk/ebooks/

Making Disciples in Messy Church
Growing faith in an all-age community
Paul Moore

'Messy Church needs to reinvent discipleship!' These words from Paul Butler, Bishop of
Southwell and Nottingham, in April 2011, may
seem alarming at first. Why does a new form
of church that has proved highly successful in
attracting unchurched families need to reinvent
Christian discipleship? What's wrong with current church methods?

The fact is, as Paul Moore (husband of Messy Church founder Lucy
Moore) points out, that current approaches are failing, leaving faith
largely theoretical and private, and giving little hope of personal motivation. This is not the way forward to more vibrant church communities.

Moore's assessment is that many assumptions need examining about
how people come to faith and about what we understand by discipleship. For all churches it is necessary to ask what is happening in the
lives of people coming to church. What wisdom can be found in scripture, Christian tradition and human experience that can help us present
the gospel in a way that encourages response?

So what does Moore think his Messy Churchgoers need, to move
them forward from Messy Church attendance to an active faith?

*First we need to facilitate more openness through positive experiences of
Christian community and building relationships and trust. Then there are
subsequent stages in which we gradually introduce people to Jesus and the
gospel, help them to take their first steps of faith and provide the right learning environment for lifelong growth in discipleship.*

These are the issues that Paul engages with in this insightful new book.
It's essential reading for Messy Church teams but will also be beneficial
for any church battling with the issues of evangelism and discipleship
in a contemporary context.

paperback, 978 0 85746 218 3, £6.99, 128 pages
Also available for Kindle: please visit www.brfonline.org.uk/ebooks/

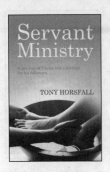

Servant Ministry
A portrait of Christ and a pattern for his followers
Tony Horsfall

The words 'servant ministry' may immediately suggest to you that this is a book just for church leaders, but stop right there. What if the term should be rightly applied to all Christians?

Tony Horsfall is convinced that an understanding of servanthood is vital for the health of local churches in this period of 'exile'—church on the fringe of society. Every member needs to appreciate their role as a servant of God, because ordinary lives that demonstrate a Christian commitment are a starting-point for engaging non-churchgoers.

In *Servant Ministry*, Tony offers a practical exposition of the first 'Servant Song' in Isaiah (42:1–9). He applies insights drawn from the passage to topics such as the motivation for service and the call to serve; valid expressions of servanthood and the link between evangelism and social action; character formation and what it means to be a servant; how to keep going over the long haul and the importance of listening to God on a daily basis, over a lifetime.

paperback, 978 085746 088 2, £7.99, 144 pages
Also available for Kindle: please visit www.brfonline.org.uk/ebooks/

To order copies of any of these books, please turn to the order form on page 155, or visit www.brfonline.org.uk.

An extract from *Spiritual Care of Dying and Bereaved People*

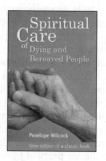

Spiritual Care of Dying and Bereaved People is a fresh, original and honest look at death and bereavement, including the author's personal experiences. Penelope Wilcock encourages readers to grow in confidence as companions, facing the questions people ask and offering a reflection on the kind of God those questions reveal. The following extract is taken from Part One of the book.

This book is about life, not death. Spending time with hospice patients in the 1980s and early '90s, the atmosphere of expectancy often struck me. When we are with people approaching death, we feel a sense of awe, the solemnity of a great moment approaching—a sacred moment...

Finding and accepting identity

Before anything else, spiritual care is about identity. Prayer, religion, philosophy, sacraments—all may play their part but, first and foremost, spiritual care is about identity.

Spirituality is all about who one is, and that is found only in relationship: with other people, the ones who make up our world, and with the foundational reality that believers call God.

For proper spiritual care to be given, there must be an affirmation of the dying or bereaved person's identity as a unique individual... as a spiritual free self, a being of dignity and worth. It is important that those who select and appoint spiritual carers look for people who regard others in that way, who will hear and see and never patronise. I am not sure that this quality in a spiritual carer can be taught: perhaps it is an awakening, a realisation, able to be recognised but not communicated... Techniques of care and listening can be taught, but not that fundamental vision of the spirituality of human encounter.

Terminal illness mounts a serious attack on the sense of identity. The powerlessness, loneliness and fear commonly experienced feel dehumanising and alienating, and constitute (or trigger) spiritual crisis in many people...

It is virtually impossible to maintain spiritual equilibrium when one's own entire being is coming apart; when physical functioning is haywire, mental processes are embarrassingly unpredictable, and emotions are ricocheting all over the place in the desperate attempt to adjust, to assimilate and to maintain the dignity of appearing normal.

The sense of self is enhanced by creating an environment for the self to live in. My choice of clothes, whether I live in a flat or a house, the fabrics and carpeting and furniture I have chosen, my ornaments and pictures and crockery, whether I eat supper at the table or curled up on the sofa with a tray on my lap, whether I decorate my home with tree and lights and tinsel at Christmas or put candles on the table for a dinner party, if I keep a cat as a companion—all of this is how I offer my identity to the world and arrive at a sense of self…

People in terminal illness often have to face the decision to sell their home. They have to find a new home for beloved pet animals that must be left behind now. In hospital they may be encouraged to wear night-clothes. The choice of how or when or what to eat is limited by the possibilities of institutional provision. No more candles on the dinner table; no longer my plates, my wallpaper, my sofa. People who appreciate enormously the care and love they are given still sit in the beds of caring institutions, saying with tears in their eyes, 'It's so hard to give up my home.' …

Good spiritual care understands that it is not things that have been lost to a terminally ill person coming into institutional care; it is the self. Like a dance or a song or a painting, the environment of home was the person's song of creation in the world: to lose it is to lose one's own space, to live in the world as a refugee…

Spiritual care involves nurturing again the bruised and diminished sense of self. This happens through the stimulus of relationship and interaction as carers bring their individual personalities to the situation, being self-expressive and self-giving without being self-indulgent…

The person's individuality and identity should be affirmed by the spiritual carer in creating a sense of not rushing, and a sense of private space in loving and respectful body language, maybe using touch. Any religious or ideological concerns of the patient should be recognised and maybe mentioned. Above all else, till the last breath, this is a person with a name, a shining light of selfhood, dust of Adam, of Eve, brought into life by the breath of the living God.

To order a copy of this book, please turn to the order form on page 155, or visit www.brfonline.org.uk.

SUPPORTING BRF'S MINISTRY

As a Christian charity, BRF is involved in seven distinct yet complementary areas.

- **BRF** (www.brf.org.uk) resources adults for their spiritual journey through Bible reading notes, books and Quiet Days. BRF also provides the infrastructure that supports our other specialist ministries.
- **Foundations21** (www.foundations21.net) provides flexible and innovative ways for individuals and groups to explore their Christian faith and discipleship through a multimedia internet-based resource.
- **Messy Church** (www.messychurch.org.uk), led by Lucy Moore, enables churches all over the UK (and increasingly abroad) to reach children and adults beyond the fringes of the church.
- **Barnabas in Churches** (www.barnabasinchurches.org.uk) helps churches to support, resource and develop their children's ministry with the under-11s more effectively .
- **Barnabas in Schools** (www.barnabasinschools.org.uk) enables primary school children and teachers to explore Christianity creatively and bring the Bible alive within RE and Collective Worship.
- **Faith in Homes** (www.faithinhomes.org.uk) supports families to explore and live out the Christian faith at home.
- **Who Let The Dads Out** (www.wholetthedadsout.org) inspires churches to engage with dads and their pre-school children.

At the heart of BRF's ministry is a desire to equip adults and children for Christian living—helping them to read and understand the Bible, explore prayer and grow as disciples of Jesus. We need your help to make an impact on the local church, local schools and the wider community.

- You could support BRF's ministry with a donation or standing order (using the response form overleaf).
- You could consider making a bequest to BRF in your will.
- You could encourage your church to support BRF as part of your church's giving to home mission—perhaps focusing on a specific area of our ministry, or a particular member of our Barnabas team.
- Most important of all, you could support BRF with your prayers.

If you would like to discuss how a specific gift or bequest could be used in the development of our ministry, please phone 01865 319700 or email enquiries@brf.org.uk.

Whatever you can do or give, we thank you for your support.

Thank you for reading BRF Bible reading notes. BRF has been producing a variety of Bible reading notes for over 90 years, helping people all over the UK and the world connect with the Bible on a personal level every day.

Could you help us find other people who would enjoy our notes?

We produce a Bible Reading Resource Pack for church groups to use to encourage regular Bible reading.

This FREE pack contains:

- Samples of all BRF Bible reading notes.
- Our Resources for Personal Bible Reading catalogue, providing all you need to know about our Bible reading notes.
- A ready-to-use church magazine feature about BRF notes.
- Ready-made sermon and all-age service ideas to help your church into the Bible (ideal for Bible Sunday events).
- And much more!

How to order your FREE pack:

- Visit: www.biblereadingnotes.org.uk/request-a-bible-reading-resources-pack/
- Telephone: 01865 319700 between 9.15 and 17.30
- Post: Complete the form below and post to: Bible Reading Resource Pack, BRF, 15 The Chambers, Vineyard, Abingdon, OX14 3FE

Name _____

Address _____

_____ Postcode _____

Telephone _____

Email _____

Please send me _____ Bible Reading Resources Pack(s)

This pack is produced free of charge for all UK addresses but, if you wish to offer a donation towards our costs, this would be appreciated. If you require a pack to be sent outside of the UK, please contact us for details of postage and packing charges. Tel: +44 1865 319700. Thank you.

BRF MINISTRY APPEAL RESPONSE FORM

Name _____

Address _____

_____ Postcode _____

Telephone _____ Email _____

Standing Order – Banker's Order
❏ I would like to support BRF's ministry with a regular donation by standing order

To the Manager, Name of Bank/Building Society
Address _____

_____ Postcode _____

Sort Code _____ Account Name _____

Account No _____

Please pay Royal Bank of Scotland plc, Drummonds, 49 Charing Cross,
London SW1A 2DX (Sort Code 16-00-38), for the account of BRF A/C No. 00774151

The sum of _____ pounds on ___/___/___ (insert date) and thereafter the same amount
on the same day each month / same day annually (delete as applic.) until further notice.

Signature _____ Date _____

Single donation
❏ I enclose my cheque/credit card/Switch card details for a donation of
£5 £10 £25 £50 £100 £250 (other) £ _____ to support BRF's ministry.

Card no. [ ][ ][ ][ ][ ][ ][ ][ ][ ][ ][ ][ ][ ][ ][ ][ ][ ][ ]

Expires [ ][ ][ ][ ]   Security code [ ][ ][ ]   Issue no. [ ][ ][ ][ ]

Signature _____ Date _____

Please use my donation for ❏ BRF ❏ Foundations21 ❏ Messy Church
❏ Barnabas Children's Ministry ❏ Faith in Homes

❏ Please send me information about making a bequest to BRF in my will.

If you would like to Gift Aid your donation, please fill in the form overleaf.

Please detach and send this completed form to: Richard Fisher, BRF,
15 The Chambers, Vineyard, Abingdon OX14 3FE. BRF is a Registered Charity (No.233280)

Bible Reading Fellowship

Please treat as Gift Aid donations all qualifying gifts of money made
today ☐   in the past 4 years ☐   in the future ☐   (tick all that apply)

I confirm I have paid or will pay an amount of Income Tax and/or Capital Gains Tax for each tax year (6 April to 5 April) that is at least equal to the amount of tax that all the charities that I donate to will reclaim on my gifts for that tax year. I understand that other taxes such as VAT or Council Tax do not qualify. I understand the charity will reclaim 28p of tax on every £1 that I gave up to 5 April 2008 and will reclaim 25p of tax on every £1 that I give on or after 6 April 2008.

Donor's details

Title _____ First name or initials _____ Surname _____

Full home address _____

_____

Postcode _____

Date _____

Signature _____

Please notify Bible Reading Fellowship if you:
• want to cancel this declaration
• change your name or home address
• no longer pay sufficient tax on your income and/or capital gains.

If you pay Income Tax at the higher or additional rate and want to receive the additional tax relief due to you, you must include all your Gift Aid donations on your Self-Assessment tax return or ask HM Revenue and Customs to adjust your tax code.

BRF PUBLICATIONS ORDER FORM

Please send me the following book(s):

		Quantity	Price	Total
169 8	The Word's Out (*D. Male & P. Weston*)	_____	£8.99	_____
218 3	Making Disciples in Messy Church (*P. Moore*)	_____	£6.99	_____
088 2	Servant Ministry (*T. Horsfall*)	_____	£7.99	_____
115 5	Spiritual Care Dying/Bereaved People (*P. Wilcock*)	_____	£9.99	_____
061 5	Family Fun for Summer (*J. Butcher*)	_____	£4.99	_____
139 1	Ten-Minute Summer Activity Book (*B. James*)	_____	£3.99	_____

Total cost of books £ _____

Donation £ _____

Postage and packing £ _____

TOTAL £ _____

POSTAGE AND PACKING CHARGES				
order value	UK	Europe	Surface	Air Mail
£7.00 & under	£1.25	£3.00	£3.50	£5.50
£7.01–£30.00	£2.25	£5.50	£6.50	£10.00
Over £30.00	free	prices on request		

Please complete the payment details below and send with payment to: **BRF, 15 The Chambers, Vineyard, Abingdon OX14 3FE**

Name _____

Address _____

_____ Postcode _____

Tel _____ Email _____

Total enclosed £ _____ (cheques should be made payable to 'BRF')

Please charge my Visa ❑ Mastercard ❑ Switch card ❑ with £ _____

Card no: ▢▢▢▢ ▢▢▢▢ ▢▢▢▢ ▢▢▢▢ ▢▢▢▢

Expires ▢▢▢▢ Security code ▢▢▢

Issue no (Switch only) ▢▢▢▢

Signature (essential if paying by credit/Switch) _____

❑ I would like to take out a subscription myself:

Your name _____

Your address _____

_____ Postcode _____

Tel _____ Email _____

Please send *Guidelines* beginning with the September 2013 / January 2014 / May 2014 issue: (delete as applicable)

(please tick box)	UK	SURFACE	AIR MAIL
GUIDELINE	❑ £15.00	❑ £21.60	❑ £24.00
GUIDELINES 3-year sub	❑ £37.80		
GUIDELINES pdf download	❑ £12.00 (UK and overseas)		

Please complete the payment details below and send with appropriate payment to: **BRF, 15 The Chambers, Vineyard, Abingdon OX14 3FE**

Total enclosed £ _____ (cheques should be made payable to 'BRF')

Please charge my Visa ❑ Mastercard ❑ Switch card ❑ with £ _____

Card no: ❑❑❑❑❑❑❑❑❑❑❑❑❑❑❑❑❑❑❑❑

Expires ❑❑❑❑ Security code ❑❑❑

Issue no (Switch only) ❑❑❑❑

Signature (essential if paying by card) _____

To set up a direct debit, please also complete the form on page 159 and send it to BRF with this form.

GUIDELINES GIFT SUBSCRIPTIONS

❑ I would like to give a gift subscription (please provide both names and
addresses:

Your name _____

Your address _____

_____ Postcode _____

Tel _____ Email _____

Gift subscription name _____

Gift subscription address _____

_____ Postcode _____

Gift message (20 words max. or include your own gift card for the recipient)

_____

_____

Please send *Guidelines* beginning with the September 2013 / January 2014 /
May 2014 issue: (delete as applicable)

(please tick box)		UK	SURFACE	AIR MAIL
GUIDELINES		❑ £15.00	❑ £21.60	❑ £24.00
GUIDELINES 3-year sub		❑ £37.80		
GUIDELINES pdf download		❑ £12.00 (UK and overseas)		

Please complete the payment details below and send with appropriate
payment to: **BRF, 15 The Chambers, Vineyard, Abingdon OX14 3FE**

Total enclosed £ _____ (cheques should be made payable to 'BRF')

Please charge my Visa ❑ Mastercard ❑ Switch card ❑ with £

Card no: ▭▭▭▭▭▭▭▭▭▭▭▭▭▭▭▭▭▭▭

Expires ▭▭▭▭ Security code ▭▭▭

Issue no (Switch only) ▭▭▭▭

Signature (essential if paying by card) _____

To set up a direct debit, please also complete the form on page 159 and send
it to BRF with this form.

DIRECT DEBIT PAYMENTS

Now you can pay for your annual subscription to BRF notes using Direct Debit. You need only give your bank details once, and the payment is made automatically every year until you cancel it. If you would like to pay by Direct Debit, please use the form opposite, entering your BRF account number under 'Reference'.

You are fully covered by the Direct Debit Guarantee:

The Direct Debit Guarantee

- This Guarantee is offered by all banks and building societies that accept instructions to pay Direct Debits.
- If there are any changes to the amount, date or frequency of your Direct Debit, The Bible Reading Fellowship will notify you 10 working days in advance of your account being debited or as otherwise agreed. If you request The Bible Reading Fellowship to collect a payment, confirmation of the amount and date will be given to you at the time of the request.
- If an error is made in the payment of your Direct Debit, by The Bible Reading Fellowship or your bank or building society, you are entitled to a full and immediate refund of the amount paid from your bank or building society.
  - – If you receive a refund you are not entitled to, you must pay it back when The Bible Reading Fellowship asks you to.
- You can cancel a Direct Debit at any time by simply contacting your bank or building society. Written confirmation may be required. Please also notify us.
